IMMIGRATION AND HIGHER EDUCATION

Institutional Responses to Changing Demographics

Maryann Jacobi Gray

Elizabeth Rolph

Elan Melamid

Supported by
The Andrew W. Mellon Foundation

Center for Research on Immigration Policy

RAND

Immigrants constitute an increasingly significant segment of the U.S. population. By 1994, more than 8 percent of the U.S. population was foreign-born, and the rate of immigration was at its highest since the 1911–1920 period. Today's growing immigrant population enters a national economy that is in transition. Most notably, future labor markets will demand more well-educated workers and fewer less-educated ones. If immigrants are to enjoy the benefits of economic assimilation and if our nation is to enjoy the fruits of a well-educated labor force, newcomers must participate fully and successfully in both K–12 and higher education.

This is one of three RAND reports that examine the participation of immigrants in the nation's educational system. Each of these reports is based on research supported by The Andrew W. Mellon Foundation.

Newcomers in American Schools: Meeting the Educational Needs of Immigrant Youth (McDonnell and Hill, 1993; MR-103-AWM/PRIP) focuses on the response of K–12 schools to the continuing increase in immigration and offers suggestions for improving education. *How Immigrants Fare in U.S. Education* (Vernez and Abrahamse, 1996, MR-718-AMF) measures the participation of immigrants in postsecondary education and the factors associated with the educational attainment of immigrant and native-born youths. Our report focuses on the effects of the continuing increase in immigration on higher education institutions, the responses of these institutions, and the reasons for their responses. Higher education administrators and policymakers and others concerned with higher education or immigration should be interested in this study.

CONTENTS

TABLES

Immigrants constitute an increasingly significant portion of the U.S. population. Almost as many immigrants legally entered the United States during the 1980s (7.3 million) as during the preceding two decades (7.8 million). This legal flow was substantially augmented by illegal immigration. Moreover, the dramatic growth in immigration over the past two decades has continued into the 1990s, with 4.5 million immigrants arriving between 1990 and 1994. By 1994, more than 8 percent of the U.S. population was foreign-born, and the rate of immigration was at its highest since the 1911–1920 period.

Today's growing immigrant population is entering a national economy that is in transition. Most notably, future labor markets will demand more well-educated workers and fewer less-educated ones. If immigrants are to enjoy the benefits of economic assimilation and if our nation is to enjoy the fruits of a well-educated labor force, newcomers must participate fully and successfully not only in K–12 but also in higher education.

However, in seeking access to and academic success within higher education, immigrants face a number of obstacles. The weak English language skills of some immigrant students pose the most serious impediment to success within higher education. Although these students' language skills may be sufficient for high-school-level work, they may be inadequate for college courses. Additionally, higher education institutions differ in the quantity and quality of English as a second language (ESL) instruction, because of constricted budgets and institutional leaders who may feel limited responsibility for helping immigrants overcome language difficulties.

Furthermore, immigrants may confront other problems, such as acculturative stress, lack of familiarity with the American higher education system, the need to balance school with family and work responsibilities, and discrimination. The experiences of native-born students have demonstrated how these factors can depress college enrollment and achievement once in college.

STUDY PURPOSE AND METHODS

Given the importance of postsecondary education for immigrants and the potential barriers to access and academic success that immigrants may face, we focus on two areas of inquiry. The first is immigrants themselves, and relevant questions include how do immigrants' college enrollment, retention, and graduation rates compare with those of native-born students; what factors hinder or facilitate college enrollment for immigrants; and are institutions meeting immigrant students' needs. The second area of inquiry focuses on institutions. Relevant questions include what challenges and opportunities does the continuing increase in immigration pose for higher education institutions; how are institutions responding to these challenges and opportunities; and why are they responding in this manner.

This report addresses the second area of inquiry only. A companion report (Vernez and Abrahamse, 1996, MR-718-AMF) addresses the first area of inquiry. Our research methods included case studies of 14 higher education institutions. Our results follow.

MAJOR FINDINGS

Immigrants Are Not a Targeted Population on the Campuses Included in This Study

Although ethnicity is a highly salient characteristic in the opinion of all campus members—students, faculty, and administration alike—neither faculty nor administrators think of *immigrant* students as a group. In their numerous data collection efforts, campuses collect little to no data on immigrant status. Similarly, in their direct dealings with students, faculty and staff report themselves rarely aware of immigrant status. Few believe that failure to distinguish this population is a shortcoming.

To the Degree Campus Faculty and Administrators Have Any Knowledge in This Area, They Believe Their Immigrant Students Generally Do Better Than Native-Born Students

When pressed, respondents typically described immigrants as doing better than other students, and although they acknowledged some possible specific barriers to academic success, they largely feel that immigrants enjoy more-than-compensating supports.

There Is Consistent Opposition to the Introduction of Special Support Programs That Target Immigrant Students

Our case studies revealed generally consistent and strong opposition to the introduction of special support programs targeting immigrant students. Respondents argued against such measures for several reasons. They believe the problems immigrants face are no different from those faced by many other students and that, in fact, there are other groups that are more disadvantaged than immigrants. Many fear growing campus fragmentation and believe that targeting groups for special support exacerbates that problem. Respondents also report that immigrant students are reluctant users of existing programs. Respondents would, therefore, not expect them to use new services that might be developed for them.

Inadequate Language Skills Are Reported as the Most Outstanding Problem Shared by Immigrants

Respondents generally agree that the greatest barrier immigrants face in acquiring a sound postsecondary education is inadequate language skills. However, the agreement ends there. There is substantial disagreement regarding how faculty should respond to such student deficiencies and what responsibilities colleges and universities have for remediation.

In Some Settings, Policies Regarding Eligibility Requirements for Admissions and Financial Aid Are Poorly Understood and Unevenly Implemented

Eligibility requirements for admission and for some forms of financial aid are a complex combination of statute, court rulings, and institutional policy, which, in recent years, has undergone substantial change. Moreover, requirements established by external bodies often conflict with institutional and staff values. The result has been uneven awareness and implementation. Respondents offered many different perspectives on whether and how these complex systems affect immigrant students.

DISCUSSION

Although immigrants are perceived as succeeding within higher education, the institutions serving them are encountering challenges linked to immigration. Left unaddressed, these challenges are likely to increase and culminate in intervention by outside policymakers.

More specifically, the continuing increase in immigration has affected higher education institutions in three ways. First, the increase in immigration strains administrative operations and functions, hindering efficiency and cost-effectiveness. For example, the increase in immigration places greater burdens on staff in admissions offices because of time-consuming and labor-intensive review of foreign transcripts. These reviews are then used to make decisions about admissions and transfer credit for immigrants who attended secondary or postsecondary school outside the United States. Workload also increases for staff who verify or clarify student residence for fee purposes, for financial aid staff, and for ESL instructors. Despite unwieldy processes in these areas, however, the schools we studied largely persist in using established procedures and often resist considering alternatives.

Second, rising immigration challenges the assumptions underlying programs designed to improve access to education or academic success among particular racial or ethnic groups. The logic of classifying all black or all Hispanic students as disadvantaged, for example, begins to break down when these groups include both immigrants with strong educational backgrounds and native-born students with relatively weak educational backgrounds. Despite growing within-group diversity linked to immigration, institutions continue to stress race and ethnicity for identifying "disadvantaged" and "under-represented" students.

Third, increased immigration brings new focus to unresolved issues related to institutions' responsibilities to their students, both within and outside the classroom. As just one example, increased immigration heightens the salience of questions about the importance of English language mastery within undergraduate education. Although most case study respondents agreed that college graduates should have strong verbal and written English skills, relatively few faculty were able or willing to adjust their teaching styles to assist students with limited proficiency in English. In addition, many faculty were reluctant to penalize immigrants who, despite communications difficulties, were able to complete the college curriculum. Thus, although English mastery is important, immigrant students with poor English skills are being passed, which reflects incongruence between institutional values and actual instructor behavior. Other unresolved issues include the role of ESL, the importance of student participation in campus activities, and institutional responsibilities toward undocumented immigrants.

These tensions carry implications for equity and program quality that go beyond concerns related solely to immigrant students, but few institutions are responding in a systematic or proactive manner. To date, the challenges to institutions posed by immigration have not achieved a level of intensity that requires concerted intervention or response, but they do create increased strain on a day-to-day basis. As immigrant enrollments increase, or as institutions experience new demands in other domains, these challenges will grow in significance.

RECOMMENDATION TO INSTITUTIONS

The dramatic growth in immigration to the United States and the critical role of higher education in promoting economic assimilation indicate that institutional leaders should focus greater attention on immigrant students. At this time, empirical data cannot confirm perceptions and beliefs about immigrant students. Needed information includes both descriptive statistics about immigrants' enrollment and retention in college, attitudinal and needs assessment studies, and evaluations of student outcomes and of the effectiveness of remedial and ESL programs. Given the importance of immigrant access to higher education, institutional leaders and educational researchers should study the effects of immigration on the educational sector and institutional responses. These responses should then be assessed for their effects on immigrants, nonimmigrant students, and the institutions themselves.

ACKNOWLEDGMENTS

We are grateful to those staff, faculty, and students within the 14 participating institutions who took the time to talk with us about their experiences and perceptions and who wish to remain anonymous. Thanks also to the institutional research office at each campus for providing us with background information and data on student enrollment and retention rates.

We also appreciate the assistance of our colleagues within RAND, especially Beth Benjamin, Lorraine McDonnell, and Georges Vernez. Their comments on earlier drafts of this manuscript were very helpful. Additionally, Allan Abrahamse's analyses of census data were helpful in planning, conducting, and presenting this research.

Finally, we wish to acknowledge The Andrew W. Mellon Foundation for its support of this project.

Chapter One

INTRODUCTION

Immigrants constitute an increasingly important segment of our country. By 1994, more than 8 percent of the U.S. population was foreign-born, and growth in immigration continues (Vernez and McCarthy, 1990). Immigrants are expected to account for as much as 25 percent of the projected growth in the U.S. labor force during the 1990s (U.S. Department of Labor, 1989; Fullerton, 1989).

Today's growing immigrant population enters a national economy in which the demand for low-skilled labor has diminished and the need for highly trained workers is growing. National projections indicate that as many as 40 percent of all jobs in the 1990s and beyond will be in professional, managerial, and technical occupations, and another 30 percent will require skilled labor. Barely 2 percent will fall into the low-skill category (Silvesti and Lukasiewicz, 1989; Vernez and McCarthy, 1990). In sum, future labor markets will demand more well-educated workers and fewer less-educated ones. Thus, if immigrants are to enjoy the benefits of economic assimilation and if the nation is to enjoy the fruits of a well-educated labor force, newcomers must participate fully and successfully not only in K–12 but also in higher education.

STUDY GOALS

Given the importance of postsecondary education for immigrants, we focus on two areas of inquiry. The first is immigrants themselves, and relevant questions include how do immigrants' college enrollment, retention, and graduation rates compare with those of native-born students; what factors hinder or facilitate college enrollment for immigrants; and are institutions meeting immigrant students' needs. Issues of concern include, for example, immigrants' language skills, academic preparation, understanding of the American higher education system, and use of and satisfaction with campus-based support services. This information may facilitate decisionmaking regarding whether there is a need for interventions to increase immigrant enrollment and retention in higher education and, if so, what types of interventions are needed.

The second area of inquiry focuses on institutions. Relevant questions include what challenges and opportunities does the continuing increase in immigration pose for higher education institutions; how are institutions responding to these challenges and opportunities; and why are they responding in this manner. Specific issues of concern include, for example, whether growing participation of immigrants is associated with increasing administrative or operational workloads, changing or higher demand for support services, increasing competition among student groups for resources and support, or modifications in institutional capacity to achieve goals related to diversity, retention, or quality of undergraduate education. This information may facilitate decisionmaking regarding whether intervention is needed to assist institutions in better managing rising applications and enrollments among immigrants and, if so, what types of interventions are needed.

Our recent research has addressed questions about both immigrants and institutions. A companion report (Vernez and Abrahamse, 1996) presents results from analyses of census data and a nationally representative survey dataset to compare immigrant and native-born prospective students' rates of college enrollment, and to determine the factors that predict participation in postsecondary education for immigrants.

This report describes results of analyses that use the institution as the level of analysis. We address three research questions:

- *How are institutions of higher education responding to growing immigrant populations?* Specifically, we intended to learn what changes in policies, programs, and procedures have been considered, or introduced, in response to growing immigration among institutions' service populations. Descriptions of precisely how institutions have responded provide the basis for further inquiry into why they have chosen these responses and what their effects might be.

- *Why are institutions choosing to respond as they are?* Institutional responses are the result of several determining factors. *Subjective* factors include awareness of the size and nature of immigrant flows, perceived needs of immigrants, and beliefs regarding the best way to deal with this particular population. *Objective* factors include resource constraints and outside incentives and disincentives for action. If policymakers want to alter institutional responses in some way, it is important that they understand what may be driving these responses. For example, if institutions know that immigrants need special, targeted remedial assistance but do not provide it because there are not enough resources, policymakers might offer targeted financial support. Furthermore, information about the issues that are important to those working in colleges and universities will assist policymakers in addressing normative questions about appropriate courses of institutional action. Finally, other institutions may also find it helpful to understand the rationales for the reactions of their neighbors and colleagues in matters that may be of consequence to them.

- *What are the apparent effects of immigration and chosen management approaches on the institutions themselves?* Meeting the challenges of increasing numbers of immigrants may be affecting the institutions and their ability to serve all students. Although our study design does not support firm conclusions about these questions, it permits us to report perceptions.

Responses to these three questions will reveal whether immigration has created new and unresolved challenges for higher education and, if so, what the nature of these challenges is. Potential problems related to the increased participation of immigration in undergraduate education stem from four areas. First, institutions may face difficulties if immigrant students need new or higher levels of support, which would therefore place new demands on institutional support services. Second, institutions may face difficulties if increasing applications or enrollments of immigrant students increase staff, faculty, or administrative workloads or otherwise strain current campus operations. Third, institutions may face difficulties stemming from the potential for community disruption and intergroup conflict created by changing demographic conditions. Fourth, institutions may face difficulties as a result of external or internal political pressures related to immigration, especially if those pressures and policies clash with those of educational leaders. The presence of such unresolved problems signals the need for policy intervention.

The choices that institutions make in responding to immigrants have important consequences for the well-being of the immigrants themselves, the higher education sector, and the nation. The ultimate goal of this study is to find effective ways to respond to the needs of the nation's growing immigrant population that realistically acknowledge the economic and political constraints postsecondary institutions face.

ANALYTIC FRAMEWORK

We have found it helpful to sharpen the focus of our research questions by applying them to the educational functions of colleges and universities that fall under the headings of access, retention and academic success, and retention and cocurricular programs.

Access

Colleges and universities promote access through programs and services in three key areas: (1) outreach and recruitment, to encourage high school students and adults to attend college and to provide information and assistance to help them successfully apply; (2) admissions, to screen applicants for eligibility for enrollment; and (3) financial aid, to allocate institutional, state, and federal loans and grants that help defray the costs of college. Because current patterns of college enrollment vary significantly across ethnic and racial groups, many institutions have developed special policies and programs across these three areas to boost college enrollment among underrepresented groups.

Retention and Academic Success

Access alone does not guarantee educational success. Because about half of all college students drop out before completing their baccalaureate programs, many institutions have also undertaken responsibility for student retention. In the past, institutions could promote retention and academic success by selecting only those students likely to complete their programs. Today, however, in an effort to increase access, institutions enroll many students who are at high risk for attrition. Thus, they have employed new strategies to help students succeed.

These strategies typically fall into two categories. Institutions may seek to bolster students' academic skills, success, and interest as a way to encourage student commitment. They may also seek to better connect high-risk students to life on campus to that same end. Programs falling into the first group include remedial courses, academic support services, English as a second language (ESL) instruction, modifications to curricula or course content, and the introduction of ethnic or multicultural studies programs.

Retention and Cocurricular Programs

A growing body of research, however, indicates that not only is retention a function of academic ability and success, but also of a student's integration into campus life (Astin, 1993; Tinto, 1987). Although the logic of the first approach may be rather transparent, the logic of the second is not. Students who feel alienated, unwelcome, or alone are less likely to become involved and engaged in the college experience and more likely to drop out. Subtle or overt signs of discrimination can create a "chilly" campus climate for minority and nontraditional students that interferes with their academic persistence and success (Pearson, Shavlik, and Touchton, 1989). Further, personal problems can distract students from their academic work and increase the likelihood of attrition. To promote integration of students into the campus community, many colleges and universities offer support services intended to help students overcome problems ranging from poor health to cultural alienation.

In addition, they support an array of student cocurricular activities (e.g., clubs, associations, fraternities) that provide alternative avenues for students to increase their commitment to and integration into higher education.

At the same time, cocurricular activities and support services are thought by many to extend the academic goals of the college. For example, participation in campus activities or use of support services is widely believed to build such life skills as leadership, teamwork, career exploration, and an ability to work with individuals of different backgrounds. These skills, in turn, help to prepare students to use their academic training in the workplace.

Organizing Questions

Within each of these domains, we pose the first three questions that underlie our research. First, we describe how higher education institutions are responding to the continuing increase in immigration, particularly with regard to the development of targeted programs, services, policies, and procedures. Second, we describe why the institutions are responding in this way. In so doing, we consider subjective perceptions, including perceptions of the *need* for and *appropriateness* of interventions targeted to immigrant students. We also consider objective constraints, such as budget or staffing, that influence institutional responses. Third, we describe the perceived effects of institutional responses on institutions and immigrants. Our final synthesis of results cuts across the domains of access, retention and academic success, and retention and cocurricular programs to discuss the extent and nature of problems related to immigration facing the higher education sector.

The next section describes how past research has informed these questions, and we then turn to the methods used in this study.

PAST RESEARCH

Existing research about immigrant students in higher education is sparse, suffers from numerous methodological weaknesses, and is often clearly advocative in nature. It does, however, suggest some challenges that institutions may encounter stemming from the continuing increase in participation of immigrants.

First, educational research indicates that, like other disadvantaged students, many immigrants must overcome the dual obstacles of financial need and lack of adequate academic preparation for college (Green, 1989; Richardson and Bender, 1985). However, immigrants differ from native-born students on a number of other dimensions. For example, Anglo-American and Hispanic students show different learning styles, which carries implications for the optimal delivery of higher education instruction and academic support services (Scarpaci and Fradd, 1985). Value differences across various cultural groups have been linked to differences between immigrant and native-born students' responses to educational programs and support services (Furnham and Alibhai, 1986). Other research indicates that immigrant students, even when academically successful, may face acculturative stress that threatens their socioemotional well-being (Graham, 1983; Mena, Padilla, and Maldonado, 1987; Pruitt, 1978; Sue and Zane, 1985). Immigrants have also written of the psychological difficulties they experienced as undergraduates (Chen and Hong, 1989). In response, Fernandez (1988) and Sodowsky and Carey (1987) recommend that university counseling services incorporate cross-cultural counseling to better serve immigrants.

Similarly, The Andrew W. Mellon Foundation *Roundtable Report on Immigrant Issues in Higher Education* (Romero, 1991) concluded that, although most colleges and universities emphasize language services for immigrant students, these students' needs are much broader. The roundtable participants recommended that institutions provide social and psychological support as well as academic remediation and assistance in understanding the U.S. higher education culture.

Other reports advocate increased institutional responsiveness to specific ethnic groups that include many immigrants, such as Hispanics or Asians in California (Asian Pacific American Education Advisory Committee, 1990; University of California Latino Eligibility Task Force, 1993). For example, a 1989 survey of students attending California State University (the nation's largest public university system) indicated that Asian American students (who included many immigrants) were more dissatisfied and alienated from the campus community than any other ethnic group (Asian Pacific American Education Advisory Committee, 1990). Similar findings emerged from a University of California student survey (Jacobi, 1989).

Second, additional insight into the potential problems facing higher education institutions as immigration increases comes from research conducted in community settings. Bach (1993) and colleagues describe how six diverse communities responded to an influx of immigrants. Results included social disorder, intergroup segregation and conflict, and economic and political restructuring. These findings underscore the fact that immigration (or other demographic changes) requires adjustment and accommodation among all members of the community, not only the newcomers. To the extent that colleges and universities are a microcosm of society, they will experience similar reactions to the continuing increase in immigration.

Third, media coverage about higher education and immigration highlights the potential political pressures that institutions may face. For example, in just over a year, *The Chronicle of Higher Education* has run news stories about higher education leaders' concerns related to such policies as a proposal to deny Pell Grants for ESL study in community colleges (September 21, 1994); California's Proposition 187, which denies undocumented immigrants access to California public higher education (February 24, 1995); slashes in federal student aid that threaten access for low-income students, including many immigrants (March 3, 1995); state funding cuts that threaten ESL programs (June 16, 1995); and proposed congressional legislation based on the Republican Party's "Contract with America" that would strip legal immigrants of eligibility for financial aid (November 3, 1995).

In addition, analyses of higher education governance and organizational behavior give cause for concern about the ability of the sector to accommodate and adapt to changes, such as an increase in immigrant students. Paramount among the problems constraining the sector is severe financial distress. State and federal surveys reveal that public and private institutions of all types have been forced to reduce expenditures, often by reducing existing programs, increasing class size, limiting enrollment, and cutting faculty and staff (Zumeta and Looney, 1994; *The Chronicle of Higher Education*, 1994 and 1995). Although the dramatic budget cuts and retrenchments of the early 1990s are leveling out, analysis indicates enduring fiscal constraints, with the result that institutions can no longer respond to new demands with new resources; instead, they must meet new demands by reallocating existing resources (Benjamin et al., 1993). The governance structures and political climate of decisionmaking in higher education, however, render such reallocations difficult for institutional leaders to implement (Clotfelter et al., 1991; Weick, 1976).

In addition to financial pressures, the struggles of higher education institutions to serve an increasingly diverse student population are well documented. For example, the growing ethnic diversity of the college student population has stimulated new questions about the responsiveness of curricula and campus social climates to a diverse population (Butler and Schmitz, 1992; Levine and Cureton, 1992). The growing disparity between the need for and supply of financial aid dollars threatens access for low-income students (Shires, 1995). Competition for limited resources coupled with debate about the responsibilities of higher education to historically underrepresented groups have fueled racial tensions and ethnic hostilities on U.S. campuses that mirror those found in the larger community (Institute for the Study of Social Change, 1991; Vernez and McCarthy, 1990).

In summary, the trends in immigration coupled with those in higher education suggest that institutions will likely experience difficulty responding to the challenges associated with immigration. As a result, institutions may be unable to meet immigrant students' needs or, in so doing, they may encounter organizational, financial, or political problems. This study attempts to determine if this is in fact occurring and, if so, to describe problems facing our nation's colleges and universities related to immigration and identify directions for resolving them.

METHODS

This study relies on case study methods, which are most appropriate for exploring the variety of responses institutions might choose and the variety of rationales underlying those responses (Yin, 1994). Our case-level data are both qualitative and quantitative and are drawn from a number of sources, including demographic data for the area from which the institutions draw students, institutional statistics, interviews with a large number of respondents in each institution, and interviews with related policymakers.

For purposes of this study, we define "immigrant" as an individual who was born in another country and has migrated to the United States. An immigrant, as defined here, includes undocumented individuals, those who have applied for asylum but have not yet had a hearing, permanent residents, and naturalized citizens. Our definition does not include children of immigrants, although some research suggests that second-generation students face substantial barriers to success in higher education (Portes and Zhou, 1994). We also exclude foreign (J-1 or F-1 visa) students, because, although many foreign students will seek to become immigrants, the institutional policies and resources that apply to foreign students differ substantially from those for immigrants.

This study focuses upon institutional responses to immigrant enrollment at the undergraduate level. Graduate and professional school students, students who are seeking vocational certificates, and students who are enrolled in courses on a noncredit basis (e.g., through university extension or continuing education services) are excluded from consideration because the policy context differs significantly from that for baccalaureate study.

Site Selection

Prior to selecting our case study sites, we conducted brief telephone surveys of a random sample of 75 institutions located in six regions of the country that are absorbing large numbers of immigrants: the New York/New Jersey metropolitan area, South Florida, Chicago, Northern California, Southern California, and Texas. Telephone interviews were conducted with the director of institutional research or a designee, usually an institutional research analyst but sometimes a student affairs administrator. The telephone surveys were intended to determine the percentage of immigrants enrolled as undergraduates and any major issues, faced by the campus, related to immigrant students.

In seeking institutions to participate as case study sites, we considered the following criteria:

- *Number of immigrants.* We sought institutions that had relatively high enrollments of immigrant students as well as a small comparison group with lower enrollments of immigrants. The telephone survey showed that slightly less than one quarter of the schools had immigrant enrollments of 12 percent or more, and we therefore used this as our criterion for "high" immigrant enrollments.

- *Characteristics of immigrants* (e.g., country of origin). We sought institutions that served various immigrant populations, including Mexican, Latin American, Caribbean, Southeast Asian, and Eastern European or Russian immigrants. We also sought institutions that served a diverse group of immigrants as well as those that served predominantly only one group of immigrants.

- *Institutional type* (e.g., public versus private, degrees granted). Although we originally sought to maximize diversity in institutional types, our pilot study indicated very few baccalaureate-granting institutions (especially private liberal arts colleges) with significant participation by immigrants. We therefore dropped this category from the study.

- *Geographic location.* Our early plans called for sampling institutions in those regions of the country absorbing the largest numbers of immigrants: Texas, California, Florida, New York, New Jersey, and Illinois. Our pilot study indicated, however, that Texas institutions faced a unique set of policy issues related to the large number of Mexican nationals crossing the border to attend college in the United States. We therefore decided to concentrate our investigations in other areas since we believed that results from these other areas would have the broadest applicability to the higher education sector generally. We did, however, conduct telephone interviews with administrators at three South Texas institutions as well as state-level educational administrators.

- *Links between community colleges and four-year institutions.* Because our focus was on undergraduate students seeking bachelors' degrees, we sought community colleges that served as "feeder schools" to nearby four-year institutions. For comparison purposes, we included one large urban community college that assigned a relatively low priority to the transfer function but included a high proportion of immigrants in its student population.

- *Tradition of serving immigrants.* We considered institutions that have served immigrants for many generations as well as those that have not historically served immigrants.

Following the pilot survey, we invited 16 institutions to participate as case study sites. Fourteen accepted. Of the two that refused, one had just appointed a new president and was undergoing a major reorganization. The leadership of that institution felt that a site visit would be disruptive. The other institution did not respond to repeated calls and letters. Thus, to the best of our knowledge, these two institutions do not differ from the participating institutions in ways that would distort or bias our analysis.

Characteristics of Sites

We studied 14 institutions in five regions of the country: Southern California, Northern California, Chicago, the New York/New Jersey metropolitan area, and South Florida. These regions cover five of the six states absorbing the largest numbers of immigrants (Texas being excluded for reasons described above). As shown in Table 1.1, these regions differ in their concentration of immigrants, but all are substantially higher than that in other parts of the nation (except Texas).

The unit of analysis for the case studies is the institution. However, four institutions had multiple campuses, so the actual number of campuses visited was 20. Enrollment in these institutions ranged

Table 1.1

Percentage of College-Age Immigrants in Study Locations

Region	Number of College-Age People (19–25)	Percentage Immigrants
Southern California	228,000	34.5
Northern California	50,294	14.9
Chicago area	770,000	13.9
New York area	478,000	20.7
South Florida	307,000	32.2

SOURCE: 1990 Census.

from a low of 14,000 students to a high of over 50,000 students. Thus, these schools were larger than most higher education institutions.

Table 1.2 describes the 14 institutions in which full-scale case studies were conducted. Five are community colleges, and nine are four-year institutions. Of the latter, four granted the masters degree as the highest offered and five offered doctoral degrees. Five institutions (two community colleges, two masters-granting universities, and one doctoral-granting university) are in California. Three (one community college and two doctoral-granting universities) are in Chicago. Three (two community colleges and one masters-granting university) are in South Florida. Two (one masters-granting and one doctoral-granting) universities are in New York, and one doctoral-granting

Table 1.2

Overview of Sites

	State	Total Enrollment[a]	Immigrants Among Undergrads (Percentage)	Strength of Tradition of Serving Immigrants
Doctoral-Granting				
Site 1	S. California	15,000–20,000	20[b]	Low
Site 2	New York	15,000–20,000	15	Medium
Site 3	New Jersey	30,000–35,000	15[b]	Medium
Site 4	Chicago	10,000–15,000	8[b]	Low
Site 5	Chicago	25,000–30,000	15[b]	High
Masters-Granting				
Site 6	Florida	20,000–25,000	25	High
Site 7	New York	15,000–20,000	20[b]	High
Site 8	S. California	25,000–30,000	15	Medium
Site 9	N. California	20,000–25,000	12	Low
Community Colleges				
Site 10	Florida	>40,000	37	High
Site 11	Florida	25,000–30,000	16	Low
Site 12	Chicago	>40,000	50	High
Site 13	S. California	20,000–25,000	25	Medium
Site 14	N. California	15,000–20,000	12[b]	Low

[a]Ranges rather than exact enrollment numbers are provided to protect the confidentiality of the sites. Enrollment figures vary across sources. These figures are derived from Higher Education Publications, 1995.

[b]Back-up documentation not available to the research team.

university is in New Jersey; all three of these institutions serve the New York/New Jersey metropolitan area. All but one institution, which was included for comparison purposes, are public.

All of the community colleges had articulation agreements with at least one of the four-year institutions in the sample; transfer rates varied, although four of the five were actively seeking to boost transfer rates. The fifth community college focused primarily upon vocational, ESL, and basic skills training, and few students transferred or aspired to the baccalaureate.

Eight of the 14 institutions provided the research team with written reports about immigrant student enrollment at the undergraduate level. Data for the other six institutions are based on telephone or in-person interviews with institutional research staff. Because we do not have documentation for the data provided in these interviews, we treat these data as estimates.

The percentage of immigrant students in the undergraduate student body ranged from 50 percent to less than 10 percent. The proportion of immigrants enrolled in these institutions would be even higher if these calculations included graduate students and/or students enrolled in courses but not seeking an undergraduate degree. Three institutions with immigrant student enrollments of 12 percent or less (one doctoral-granting, one masters-granting, and one community college) were included for comparison purposes.

California institutions included predominantly Asian and Hispanic (Mexican and Latin American) immigrants, although one California institution in the sample also served several hundred Russian immigrants. Chicago institutions enrolled a diverse immigrant population, although the universities enrolled predominantly Hispanic (Mexican) and Southeast Asian immigrants while the community college enrolled a majority of Russian immigrants. The East Coast institutions all enrolled substantial numbers of Caribbean immigrants, and Florida institutions also included Latin American immigrants.[1]

---

[1] In addition to the 14 primary sites, we also conducted smaller-scale case studies at another six institutions. Of the six institutions where more limited visits were made, four were community colleges, one was a masters-granting university, and one was a

Case Study Procedures

We spent two to three days at each institution, talking with 8 to 20 individuals at each. Respondents included administrators and staff from the academic and student services areas, faculty, and students. In each site, we sought interviews with respondents from the following: (1) admissions and outreach; (2) financial aid; (3) student activities; (4) academic, psychological, or career counseling; (5) academic support services; (6) English as a second language; (7) faculty senate; (8) office of the vice president for academic affairs/provost; and (9) the institutional research office. In consultation with the designated liaison at each campus, we arranged additional interviews as appropriate with the president or chancellor, faculty and department chairs, student affairs vice president, foreign students' coordinator, or the director of the multicultural center. We also moderated focus groups with students on five campuses and held individual interviews with students on another four campuses.[2] Table 1.3 shows the number and distribution of interviews conducted.

We used semistructured interview guidelines throughout the case studies, with slight variations in the guidelines for different functions or departments. Among the issues investigated were the following:

- perceived trends in immigrant student enrollments and characteristics

- any student issues relevant to immigrants the institution was facing

---

research university. These smaller-scale visits are not discussed further and primarily provided background information and pilot-testing opportunities. In addition, we conducted telephone interviews with representatives of three public institutions in Texas. These interviews provided contextual information and afforded an opportunity to confirm that the findings reported here largely apply to Texas as well. Detailed results of these telephone interviews are not included in this report.

[2]Student participants were selected by the site liaisons and results cannot be considered representative of all immigrant students. Nonetheless, the student voices add an important dimension to this study and allowed us to assess the congruence between faculty and staff perceptions on the one hand and those of at least some students on the other.

Table 1.3

Number and Distribution of Interviews

Type of Respondent	Number of Interviews
Academic administrator[a]	21
Student affairs administrator[b]	18
Faculty senate president or chair	5
Faculty in academic discipline	16
ESL instructor or faculty	18
Admissions director or staff[c]	18
Financial aid director or staff	14
Academic support staff	19
Student services/activities staff	31
Institutional research	14
Students (individual interviews)	4
Students (focus group interviews)	23
Other staff or administrators	9
Total	210

[a]Includes deans and above, including president/chancellor.

[b]Includes deans through vice president/vice chancellor.

[c]Includes outreach, equal opportunity, and student affirmative action programs.

- the degree to which campus leaders focused on immigrants in planning, policy development, program design, or student tracking or assessment

- perceived needs of immigrant students and the differences between their needs and those of other students

- perceived responsiveness of the campus to immigrant student needs and interests

- the degree to which efforts to serve immigrants compete with efforts to serve other disadvantaged groups

- the nature of the challenges and opportunities that the continuing increase in immigration may create for the institution.

All case studies were conducted during the 1993–94 academic year. Interviews lasted between 60 and 120 minutes. We guaranteed confidentiality of both individual participants and institutions, inviting respondents to speak freely about the challenges and opportunities facing their institution related to the continuing increase in immigration.

Interviews were summarized in a narrative form using a standard format. These summaries were then coded using a specially designed set of codes that related to the major research questions. A computerized qualitative data analysis system was used to extract the major themes across institutions and compare states and institutional types.

While interviewing was the predominant means of data collection, we also collected relevant documentation from the campuses, including, as available, course catalogs, institutional fact books, and special reports (e.g., reports of institutional task forces, campus "climate" surveys, or strategic plans).

Caveats and Limitations of the Methodology

We cannot determine the extent to which the findings described here apply to institutions that were not included in the sample. Our intent, however, was not to obtain data representative of the higher education sector overall but rather to identify the critical issues and challenges that institutions are likely to confront in response to the continuing increase in immigration in their communities and on their campuses.

To achieve our goal of describing how institutions are responding to increased immigration, it was necessary to explore educational decisionmakers' subjective *perceptions* of immigrant student needs and institutional responsibilities. We emphasize that such perceptions may or may not be true. For example, some respondents held incorrect or stereotypic views of some immigrant groups. Some respondents misunderstood institutional or state policies. Because these beliefs and perceptions affect institutional responses to immigrants, they were important to explore in this study. They do not, however, provide a full or unbiased picture of either immigrants or institutions.

Finally, during the time period of this study, the political context related to immigration changed significantly. Such events as the passage of Proposition 187 in California or the federal government's decision to no longer grant asylum to all Cuban refugees certainly increased public awareness of immigration issues and probably changed the nature of discussion and decisionmaking regarding immigrant student issues within higher education in important ways.

Chapter Two

THE HIGHER EDUCATION CONTEXT

The effects of immigration upon higher education institutions must be considered within the broad context of the national effects of the continuing increase in immigration and the structure of the higher education system. This chapter provides some background information about higher education, immigration to the United States, and immigrants in higher education.

HIGHER EDUCATION

The U.S. higher education sector has a three-part mission: education, research, and service. This section provides a brief overview of those aspects of the sector relevant to our research, including institutions, students, programs, and the tensions between access, retention, and academic quality.

Overview of the Sector

The higher education sector includes 3,638 institutions distributed across the country. About 45 percent of these institutions are public (state-sponsored and supported), and about 55 percent are private. Between 40 and 50 percent of higher education institutions are community colleges that offer associate of arts degrees or vocational certificates; the remainder grant bachelors' degrees or beyond. Enrollments vary from under 2,000 students (about 11 percent of institutions) to over 20,000 students (about 4 percent of institutions) (*The Chronicle of Higher Education*, 1994).

Governance and finance structures differ across states and across systems within states. Institutions maintain considerable autonomy stemming from the traditions of faculty self-governance and academic freedom. State government, however, plays a major role in public higher education. In addition to allocating funds to public colleges and universities, state-appointed boards of regents and trustees may oversee public institutions and contribute to policymaking on a wide range of issues. Most states also have some form of coordinating or governing boards, with varying levels of authority. State courts hear cases related to higher education policy. At the federal level, the government makes its primary contribution to undergraduate education by providing funds for financial aid, although legislative decisions and the federal courts also exercise some influence over the sector.

Roughly 14 million students are enrolled in higher education institutions, either full-time or part-time. Most (87 percent) are undergraduate students. Of these, about 45 percent are attending community colleges, and about 80 percent are enrolled in public institutions. Nationwide, 5 percent of undergraduate students are Asian American, 10 percent are African American, 7 percent are Hispanic, 75 percent are Anglo-American, 1 percent are American Indian, and 2 percent are foreign (*The Chronicle of Higher Education*, 1994).

Higher education institutions categorize students in many different ways. Among those breakdowns relevant to the current investigation of immigration are the following:

- *Residents versus nonresidents.* This distinction applies to public institutions only. Students meeting the criteria for state residency can pay in-state (subsidized) tuition and fees. Nonresidents (including out-of-state students, foreign students, and, in some states, undocumented immigrants or others without permanent resident status) must pay substantially higher tuition and fees and may also face more selective or stringent criteria for admissions. Note that institutional definitions of residency may or may not match definitions of residency used by other state agencies or organizations.

- *Domestic versus foreign (visa) students.* Domestic students generally include U.S. citizens and permanent residents. Foreign students are those attending college on a temporary student visa (usually F-1 or J-1). These students typically pay nonresident tuition and fees. Students with a visa generate revenue for public institutions and represent new markets for some private institutions. In addition, most higher education administrators believe that the participation of students with a visa enhances higher education by contributing to a multicultural campus climate. As a result, many colleges actively recruit students with a visa, sometimes providing dedicated support services ranging from social programs to intensive English language instruction.

- *Students eligible for special support services, including affirmative action, equal opportunity, educational equity, and other programs.* Higher education institutions sponsor a wide variety of initiatives through which they strive to increase access and equity by targeting support services to students who are from historically underrepresented groups within higher education and/or who are at increased risk of attrition. Students who meet eligibility criteria for these programs may receive targeted outreach starting in high school or before, as well as special assistance in admissions, financial aid, registration for courses, academic counseling, and tutoring. The criteria used to target students for these programs vary but may include membership in a historically underrepresented ethnic or racial group, especially but not exclusively African American, American Indian, and Hispanic; low income; attending a high school that sends few students to college and offers a limited precollege curriculum; first in one's family to attend college; and other characteristics (e.g., disabled or from a migrant family).

- *Regularly versus specially admitted students.* Regularly admitted students are those who meet institutional criteria for admissions and enrollment. Specially admitted students are those who do not meet all the requirements. For example, students' test scores may be below the published cutoffs for admissions, or they may not have completed all the courses required as part of a precollege curriculum. Many public institutions accept a limited number of students who fail to meet the standard admissions criteria as a means of promoting access for students with special talents (e.g., musicians or athletes) or promise (e.g., bright youth who did not have the opportunity to enroll in a precollege curriculum in high school). Recent immigrants with limited English proficiency who score high on the math Scholastic Achievement Test (SAT) but low on the verbal SAT, for example, may be admitted under these programs. Students admitted through special programs such as those described above may or may not be specially admitted, since many meet minimal requirements for admission.

- *Native freshmen versus transfers.* Native freshmen are those who begin undergraduate study as freshmen at the institution. Transfers are those who enter the institution after completing part of their baccalaureate program at another college or university, such as a community college. Fewer than half of all students entering community colleges in fact transfer to four-year institutions (Grubb, 1992). To increase transfer rates, community colleges and four-year public institutions in many states have developed "articulation agreements" that specify the admissions criteria for transfer students and also spell out the community college courses that can be applied toward the degree requirements of four-year institutions.

A Dominant Policy Issue: Balancing Access and Rigor

One of the major challenges confronting higher education as a sector is to balance the goals of enhancing access on the one hand and strengthening the outcomes of undergraduate education on the other (Byron, 1991; Hauptman, 1992; Richardson and Skinner, 1991). Despite overall gains in the proportion of high school graduates attending college, concerns about access continue because of disparities in college enrollment across ethnic groups, the rising costs of college, and the fact that the workplace increasingly demands college-level skills (The Aspen Institute, 1992). In practice, achieving access goals has meant that many institutions admit students who are not academically prepared for college-level course work (Garland and Grace, 1993).[1] At the same time, many institutions are striving to

---

[1]In fact, students who meet all formal eligibility requirements for admissions to public institutions may be considered "underprepared" based on placement tests or other assessments after admission. The nation's largest public university system, California

strengthen the skills and knowledge of baccalaureate recipients in response to increasing concern about the quality of undergraduate education both within and outside the academy (Finn, 1992; Gutmann, 1991). In admitting underprepared students, however, institutions increase the challenges they face in raising the overall skill levels of graduates since underprepared students have more ground to cover.

One way to resolve the tension between these two goals is to admit a broad range of students but dismiss those who fail to achieve at some minimally acceptable level. To upgrade the skill levels of graduates, institutions can raise their minimal graduation standards, so that those currently graduating at the bottom of the distribution would not be awarded the baccalaureate. However, most institutions are also striving to improve student retention and graduation rates as critical steps in increasing educational equity and in fulfilling the promise of access to admission (American Association of State Colleges and Universities, 1992; Kinnick and Ricks, 1993).[2] Thus, this solution is at best only a partial, and often unsatisfying, response to achieving the dual goals of access and strong educational standards.

The provision of academic support services, such as remedial courses, tutoring, and summer "bridge" programs for incoming freshmen, has emerged as a key strategy for achieving both goals. Through such services, institutions strive to improve retention and academic performance of underprepared students, thereby achieving both access and academic excellence. Note, however, that empirical evidence about the efficacy of remedial and support services is inconclusive, and educators disagree widely about how to set and measure standards for undergraduate education (Bers, 1994; Harvey and Green, 1993; Pascarella and Terenzini, 1991; Pike, 1992).

State University (CSU), for example, serves the top one-third of high school graduates in the state. Nonetheless, a recent report indicated that 47 percent of CSU incoming freshmen were unprepared for college-level math, and 49 percent were unprepared for college-level English (although much smaller percentages actually enrolled in remedial courses) (Wallace, 1995).

[2]Moreover, a high dropout rate is arguably inefficient since students who do not complete their bachelor's program will nonetheless accrue debt, and institutions will invest substantial resources in serving these students.

Moreover, in an era of constrained resources, institutions cannot easily respond to new student needs, such as those that might be presented by immigrant students, with new resources for support services and remediation. They must instead stretch the scope of existing services or reallocate funds, thereby forcing leaders to make trade-offs among different student groups or institutional needs and among goals (Benjamin et al., 1993).

IMMIGRATION

Nearly ten million immigrants entered the United States during the 1980s, the largest number in our nation's history. Another 4.5 million arrived between 1990 and 1994. By 1994, 22 million U.S. residents were foreign-born, representing 8.5 percent of the U.S. population. By comparison, immigrants constituted 5.4 percent of the population in 1960 (Bureau of the Census, 1993).

Almost as many immigrants legally entered the United States during the 1980s (7.3 million) as during the preceding two decades (7.8 million [U.S. Department of Justice, 1991]). The Immigration Act of 1990 (Public Law 101-649) determined the number of visas available for legal immigration (700,000 per year in fiscal 1994 and 675,000 in fiscal 1995, for example) and established a system for granting visas that sets aside the majority of visas for those with relatives in the United States, followed by "employment-based immigrants" who have the ability to contribute to the national economy, and "diversity immigrants" from nations that received relatively few visas in past years (Dunlap, 1993).

This legal flow is substantially augmented by illegal immigration (Warren, 1994). The Immigration and Naturalization Service (INS) estimates that 3.4 million undocumented immigrants resided in the United States in 1992, with almost 300,000 more projected to enter the country each year (Dunlap and Morse, 1995; Immigrant Policy Project, 1994).

Not only is the immigrant population growing, but it diverges in important ways from prior waves of immigrants. Whereas in the past most immigrants came from European nations, well over 80 percent of those who immigrated during the 1980s originated in the non-European countries of Asia, Mexico, and Central America. Large numbers also come from the former Soviet Union, the Caribbean (especially the Dominican Republic and Jamaica), and middle eastern nations (Dunlap, 1993). Thus, immigrants today face cultural discontinuities that, for many, pose significant barriers to successful participation in education in the United States.

A large fraction of recent immigrants is young and therefore school-bound at some level. For example, 24 percent of those who entered the country between 1960 and 1980 were younger than 15 years of age, the highest proportion in this age category in the history of U.S. immigration (U.S. Department of Justice, 1991). On average, newcomers are less well-educated relative to the native-born population than their predecessors (Borjas, 1990). For example, 1990 census data indicate that about 26 percent of immigrants over age 25 had less than a 9th grade education, compared with 9 percent of native-born adults (Bureau of the Census, 1993).

A large proportion of immigrants are low-income and thus would need financial aid to attend college. Fifteen percent of immigrant families lived in poverty in 1989, compared with under 10 percent of native-born families (Bureau of the Census, 1993).

A final important characteristic of the current immigrant population is its tendency to concentrate in a few locations, potentially magnifying institutional problems of support. Over 70 percent of all immigrants who entered the country in the 1980s intended to settle in only six of the 50 states—California, Florida, Illinois, New Jersey, New York, and Texas. Over 30 percent settled in California alone. These characteristics foreshadow special consequences for the nation's educational institutions.

IMMIGRANTS IN HIGHER EDUCATION

Recent RAND research has explored the actual participation of immigrants in higher education, based on census data and analyses of "High School and Beyond," a nationally representative survey dataset based on youth attending high school in the early 1980s. This research indicates that, among high school graduates, immigrants are more likely than native-born youth to enroll in a precollege curriculum, attend college, and persist in college (Vernez and

Abrahamse, 1996).[3] For example, "High School and Beyond" data reveal that 68 percent of immigrant high school graduates, compared with only 60 percent of native-born high school graduates, enrolled in college. Over one-fifth (22 percent) of immigrants in the sample completed at least 42 months of college compared with only 16 percent of native-born students. Census data, which are more current but less detailed than "High School and Beyond" results, are consistent with these findings. For example, the 1990 Census indicates that 65 percent of immigrants aged 18–21, compared with only 57 percent of native-born students in the same age group, were "in school," which could include adult and vocational school in addition to college.

These patterns hold across all ethnic groups studied, including Asian, black, Hispanic, and white. Breakdowns of Census data by country of origin, however, suggest that Mexican immigrants are less likely than native-born Mexican Americans to participate in postsecondary education. Only 44 percent of Mexican immigrants, compared with 52 percent of native-born Mexican Americans were "in school" in 1990.[4]

Thus, we find little cause for concern that those immigrants who manage to graduate from high school are being systematically excluded from the higher education or postsecondary sectors; indeed, those immigrants who persist in secondary school through graduation are more likely than native-born students to gain access to American postsecondary education. Clearly, immigrants represent a significant, and growing, share of the higher education "market."

The enrollment of immigrants in higher education institutions, however, is variable because immigrants are not evenly distributed throughout the nation. The result is that colleges and universities in areas that are absorbing substantial numbers of immigrants are most

---

[3]The high secondary school dropout rate for Hispanics indicates that, if the entire population rather than only the population of high school graduates is considered, college enrollment rates for immigrants would be lower than those for native-born people. Since high school graduation is a requirement for participation in higher education, these analyses focused on college enrollment rates among those eligible to attend.

[4]In contrast, immigrants aged 18–21 were more likely than native-born youths to be "in school" in 1990.

affected by the continuing increase in immigration and most likely to experience a sharp jump in immigrant student enrollments. The higher education sector in California is likely to experience the most substantial impacts of immigration since more than one in four (27.5 percent) of the 18–21 year old population in the state was foreign-born in 1990 (Vernez and Abrahamse, 1996). However, even outside of those regions of the country absorbing the largest number of immigrants, we find small immigrant enclaves that may dramatically change the demographic characteristics of the local college-student population. And future waves of immigrants may settle in areas that currently have only a small proportion of immigrants within their local population.

Those institutions that are serving a growing immigrant population are likely to be affected by the changing student demographics. On the one hand, increasing participation of immigrants brings important opportunities to enrich the campus environment and educational programs by incorporating diverse cultures and perspectives. On the other hand, changing student demographics may create new institutional challenges and new demands for adaptation by faculty and administrators. For example, increased participation by immigrants may have implications for patterns of student participation in academic programs, support services, and campus activities. Immigrant participation may influence intergroup relations on campus and raise new questions about how to fairly distribute resources and services.

The effects of immigration on colleges and universities will vary depending on the characteristics of the immigrants they serve. The number of countries of origin that account for at least 100,000 foreign-born residents in the United States rose from 27 in 1980 to 41 in 1991. Moreover, as with those who are native born, immigrants participating in higher education vary by ethnicity, with Hispanics least likely to enroll in college and Asians most likely to do so (Vernez and Abrahamse, 1996). Thus, some schools will face the challenge of serving a highly diverse immigrant population; others will encounter a relatively homogeneous immigrant population. Some will serve immigrants with significant academic deficits and little family or cultural tradition of participation in higher education; others will serve immigrants who are well-prepared for college and come from highly educated families.

In sum, immigrants participate in U.S. higher education at rates slightly exceeding those of the native-born population if one limits the comparison to high school graduates. The effects of immigration on higher education are uneven, however, and vary as a function of geographic factors and the characteristics of local immigrant populations. Those schools absorbing large numbers of immigrants may experience adaptive stresses, particularly if immigrants bring new needs, interests, or goals to the sector.

Constraints and Influences on Institutional Responses to Immigration

Public policy offers relatively few constraints on institutional responses to immigrants who have attained permanent resident status, but it offers substantial constraints on institutional responses to immigrants who are not permanent residents. These policies are derived from legislative action and judicial decisions related to the eligibility of students for residency status and, hence, in-state tuition and fees. Residency policies tend to be highly complex, vary significantly across states, and are enforced irregularly (Olivas, 1992). Although such policies are typically established by state legislatures or institutions, they have come under judicial review in at least three states (California, Arizona, and Illinois), and other institutions have changed their residency policies in response to potential legal challenges (e.g., City University of New York and Middlesex, Massachusetts, community colleges) (Olivas, 1992; Roos, 1991).

The case of California demonstrates the complexity and recent instability of residency policies. Prior to 1984, the state Education Code prohibited undocumented aliens from obtaining residency status. In 1985, however, the Alameda Superior Court ruled in *Leticia A. et al v. Regents of the University of California* that undocumented aliens were eligible for residency status and thus could be charged in-state tuition and fees at state institutions if they met other criteria for state residency. This decision was reversed in 1990, when the court held in *Regents of the University of California v. Bradford* that undocumented aliens were not eligible for California residency. For several years following the Bradford decision, the University of California and California Community Colleges classified undocumented immigrants as nonresident students, while California State

University continued to classify undocumented students as state residents provided they met other conditions of residency. Recently, however, a state appellate court has ruled that California State University must also charge out-of-state tuition to undocumented students (Lively, 1995).

Beyond these judicial decisions, policymakers appear to be paying increased attention to the effects of immigration upon higher education. For example, Proposition 187, passed in California and now undergoing judicial review, denies undocumented individuals the right to use publicly funded social services including higher education. Legislation that would deny or restrict financial aid for legal immigrants has been debated in Congress. And the Department of Education has considered whether to bar the use of Pell Grants for ESL instruction (Zook, 1994). At this time, however, federal financial aid policies render permanent residents fully eligible for all forms of federal financial aid.

Even without specific legislation or judicial action, institutional response to immigrants is also being constrained or influenced by political pressure and advocacy activities. Anti-immigrant sentiment is spreading, establishing a social context that raises the political risks associated with strong advocacy on behalf of immigrants.

For the most part, however, institutions have not experienced direct advocacy or political pressures related to immigrant students. Student advocacy activities focus predominantly on the needs and concerns of specific ethnic or racial groups rather than immigrants (an exception, however, was student activity surrounding the Proposition 187 election in California). Community-based immigrant advocacy groups have also focused more on issues of employment, social services, and K–12 education rather than of higher education.

Lack of Focus on Immigrants

Immigration has not emerged as a policy issue for most higher education institutions and leaders. All of the institutions in our sample lacked formal goals or plans for immigrant student access and retention. None faced mandates or accountability pressures related to immigrants. When approached about participating in our case study, several respondents noted that we were the first people to ever ask them about immigrant students.

The general lack of attention regarding immigrant students is arguably justified because immigrants are perceived to be similar to native-born students in enrollment and persistence in college. Also, institutional policies and practices do not appear to have disproportionately depressed access to higher education and academic success among immigrants as compared with native-born students.

However, we know little about the effects of immigrants on higher education institutions. In choosing not to attend to immigrants as a group, administrators may be missing some subtle effects of immigration upon educational programs and operations. This, then, became the focus of our inquiry.

Lack of Data About Immigrants

Compared with other groups of students, very little information is available about immigrant students in higher education institutions. None of the institutions were able to obtain data that replicate the definition of immigrant as "foreign-born" used in this study because none were able to differentiate naturalized citizens from those who are native-born.

Only 8 of 14 institutions we visited were able or willing to provide the research team with any statistical data about immigrant student (permanent resident or refugee) enrollments, and only two routinely reviewed enrollment data about immigrant students.

Only two provided usable information about immigrant students' countries of origin. Some institutions provided data that were essentially uninterpretable—for example, one school provided a table on students' country of origin, but data were missing for 91 percent of undergraduates. Two others, both with large foreign student populations, provided data about "noncitizens" but were unable to differentiate students who have a visa from immigrants.

Among the data we sought for this study from participating institutions were length of time immigrants had lived in the United States, retention and graduation rates for immigrants versus native-born students, trends in enrollment in ESL courses, and trends in scores on the College Board's Test of English as a Foreign Language. For each item, at most three institutions were (and in some cases no institution was) able to provide this information. Not one routinely generated reports of such information. Moreover, the available data were poorly suited to cross-institutional aggregation or comparison.

The lack of information and lack of administrative focus on immigrants are, of course, interrelated. Until administrators perceive some cause for concern, they are unlikely to request data about immigrant students; however, without data, issues related to immigrants may never become apparent. Thus, by bringing these issues to administrators' attention, this report may stimulate administrators to collect or analyze data about immigrant students in their institutions.

Overall Positive Context

Most of the discussion that follows describes the problems and challenges that institutions encounter as a result of the continuing increase in immigration. However, so that readers do not receive the impression that the effects of immigration are predominantly negative, we want to emphasize that the majority of respondents perceived the benefits of increased participation of immigrants to outweigh the problems and costs. Almost every respondent mentioned that immigrant students contribute to the diversity of the campus community, providing *all* students with valuable opportunities for cross-cultural communication and cooperation, which were considered vital skills in today's global economy. Additionally, immigrant students were perceived as highly motivated, hardworking, and often more appreciative of a college education than native-born students. Finally, respondents from a small number of colleges mentioned that immigrants represent a new and growing market that could help the school increase enrollments.

Chapter Three

IMMIGRANT ACCESS TO HIGHER EDUCATION

Ensuring qualified residents access to higher education has been a goal of state and federal education policy at least since passage of the GI bill in 1944. Proportionately more Americans participate in higher education than do citizens of any other nation (Hauptman, 1992); now over 60 percent of the nation's high school graduates attend college (*The Chronicle of Higher Education*, 1995). Nonetheless, concerns regarding access continue, particularly in light of uneven participation rates across population groups, with low-income and minority students less likely to attend college than middle or upper income, white, or Asian students (Carter and Wilson, 1995; Koretz, 1990). More recently, growth in the college-age population, particularly in states such as California that are absorbing large numbers of immigrants, coupled with declines in funding for public colleges and universities suggest that a growing gap between the number of students who are eligible for higher education and the availability of enrollment spaces will reduce participation rates for all groups, but especially for low and middle income students (Breneman, 1995; Shires, 1995). At the same time, public dissatisfaction with the quality of undergraduate instruction and student outcomes has fueled concern that the price of extending opportunities for higher education has been declining standards of instruction and the erosion of educational excellence (Bloom, 1987; Finn, 1992; Nettles, 1995).

ACCESS: ISSUES AND STRATEGIES

Despite several decades of policy attention to access, there is no consensus on definition of or measurement of access. The concept emerges from the assumption that individuals and groups face barriers to participation in higher education that are related to such factors as income, race or ethnicity, gender, disability, educational preparation, and, it is sometimes argued, even motivation or "folk" beliefs (Eaton, 1992).[1] Thus, as a matter of equity and/or efficiency, public and private actions should counter these barriers.

This report uses a relatively narrow definition of access. We focus on student participation in higher education, without regard to institutional type (Hauptman and McLaughlin, 1992). Furthermore, although most colleges and universities today agree that their responsibilities to students extend beyond admissions to facilitating retention and graduation, we limit our discussion of access in this chapter, using it as a "front-end" concept that captures the enrollment process. Subsequent chapters in this report discuss the "back-end" concept of academic success, which is necessary for retention and graduation.

Institutional activities intended to promote student access to higher education fall into three categories: outreach and recruitment, admissions, and financial aid.

Outreach and Recruitment

Outreach activities are intended to attract students to the higher education sector and also to particular institutions within the sector. Because all types of institutions compete for students, almost all have outreach programs and services in place to market themselves to prospective high school, and sometimes adult and community college, students. In addition, most institutions are committed to increasing enrollments of designated underrepresented students on their own campuses and offer focused outreach services to low-income and minority students. These services are designed to motivate students to attend college, improve their preparation, and assist them in negotiating the admissions and financial aid processes.

---

[1]Eaton, for example, describes the evolution of conceptualizations of access, ranging from a sole focus on financial obstacles to a richer concept that considers finances in combination with other obstacles, such as race and gender, academic preparation, and motivation. Cultural factors, other than those related to race and ethnicity, have not yet been widely acknowledged as barriers to access.

Admissions

Admissions activities include developing and implementing application criteria and procedures and managing the selection process. Admissions policies may be constructed to facilitate access for historically underrepresented groups, such as ethnic minority students. For example, policies that enable public institutions to admit a small number of students who do not meet the traditional entry requirements also can be used as a tool to facilitate access among underprepared students who show promise and potential for success.

Because admissions criteria that promote access and equity often result in the enrollment of students in need of remediation, tension will exist at institutions between the goal of access and the goal of educational excellence. Such tensions are exacerbated by the current fiscal and political climate. For example, the recent vote of the University of California Regents to eliminate race as a factor in admissions is related to concern that equal access has been emphasized at the expense of other goals.

Financial Aid

Financial aid programs help students overcome financial obstacles to college enrollment. Although the United States has a long history of merit-based aid, need-based aid was introduced in the 1950s (National Research Council, 1993). Students seeking access to higher education today may obtain any or all of three types of aid: gift aid, such as scholarships and grants that do not need to be repaid; loans; and jobs (e.g., work-study programs). Federal and state governments, institutions, and other private organizations (e.g., foundations) all provide aid to college students (National Research Council, 1993). This chapter focuses primarily on need-based aid, since this is the primary strategy for promoting access for individuals facing barriers to college enrollment related to finances. In 1991–92, close to $31 billion in aid was distributed, about three-quarters of which came from the federal government (National Research Council, 1993). Over half of all college students received some financial aid (National Research Council, 1993).

Immigrants as a Target Population

Immigrants typically have a number of characteristics that suggest they may be unduly disadvantaged in the competition for access to colleges and universities, and many observers of and participants in higher education have accepted the assumption that immigrants merit special attention as a group (Kerschner, 1992; Romero, 1991). Historically, students from low-income families, those who are the first in their families to attend college, American Indians, blacks, and Hispanics have been identified as underrepresented groups in the college population. Immigrants, too, are largely low-income and nonwhite. Furthermore, since immigrants are new to this country, they might not be aware of the importance of higher education to future economic success. Those from families and cultures without a strong tradition of higher education may face cultural barriers to college enrollment. In a more practical vein, immigrants are likely to face an unfamiliar and confusing array of application requirements, forms, and deadlines. Poor English skills are likely to increase the difficulty of seeking information, understanding advice from high school and college counselors, and filing admissions and financial aid applications.

Given their broad goals, colleges and universities must determine whether immigrants face serious obstacles to access and, if they do, to what extent the institutions should provide special assistance. This chapter describes how the campuses we studied are responding to the continuing increase in immigration in their service area with targeted assistance in outreach and recruitment, admissions, and financial aid. It then explores the factors that seem to be shaping their response.

INSTITUTIONAL RESPONSES TO IMMIGRATION

The colleges and universities we studied all had existing programs to extend access for underrepresented groups. In general, these institutions tended to rely on existing programs to meet the more particular needs of immigrants.

Outreach and Recruitment[2]

Institutions varied widely in the aggressiveness of their outreach activities. At a minimum, outreach or admissions staff visited local high schools and also recruited students through the use of direct mail or other advertising. Beyond this, most sponsored at least a few programs to attract and serve designated populations. These programs were especially well developed in four-year institutions; in contrast, community colleges tended to rely on mass advertising, school visits, low tuition and fees, and open admission policies to attract diverse cohorts of students.

For the most part, the continuing increase in immigration has had little effect on outreach and recruitment activities. Respondents at seven institutions we visited were unable to identify any special outreach services or activities for immigrants. Another four institutions offered very limited outreach services to immigrants—these schools had translated informational materials about the college into a variety of foreign languages and advertised in foreign language media.

Only three schools recruited immigrants for degree-granting programs. One university, for example, hired a Cambodian counselor to spend time working with Cambodian students at local high schools, encouraging them to seek a college education and helping them manage the paperwork involved in applying for admissions and financial aid.[3]

---

[2]Note that this report defines "outreach" as the array of services, programs, and activities intended to raise prospective students' awareness of, interest in, preparation for, admission to, and enrollment in a given college. We therefore consider programs such as "student affirmative action" to be part of outreach, because they strive to promote college enrollment among certain groups. We recognize, however, that such programs may be organizationally distinct from a college "outreach office" that engages in a more limited set of activities. Such programs also may have a mission that extends beyond promoting college enrollment to encompass retention and graduation.

[3]Outside of the core group of the 14 schools studied, a community college we visited in Southern California worked closely with a nearby high school with a predominantly Hispanic student body and a large number of first-generation immigrants (both Hispanic and Asian). College outreach and admissions staff visited the high school to raise students' awareness about college, to administer placement tests, and to actually enroll students in community college courses for the semester following their high school graduation. This community college also engaged in active outreach to parents and community members and sponsored special multilingual events for parents on the campus intended to inform them about the advantages of postsecondary educa-

In addition, at least four schools in the sample had attempted, with mixed success, to reach immigrant parents to encourage families to seek a college education for their children, to familiarize them with the U.S. system of higher education, and to increase their comfort level with the school. These events were intended both to build family support for college enrollment among youth by providing families with information and support that would reduce stress and improve student retention following enrollment in college. Also, it was common for colleges and universities to hold on-campus orientation sessions in the language of the target population, usually Spanish.[4]

Admissions

A wide array of policies and practices govern the admissions process. Some policies may be the product of legislatures or other funding sources, but most are developed at the system or institutional level. They are subject to frequent review as institutions strive to improve efficiency and to balance the goals of increasing enrollments, increasing the enrollments of certain populations, and increasing or maintaining student preparation and quality.

Of particular relevance to immigrants are state and systemwide policies that distinguish between in-state and out-of-state residents. Public institutions typically subsidize tuition and fees for in-state residents, while requiring out-of-state residents to meet more stringent admissions standards as well as to pay substantially higher tuition and fees.

Colleges and universities themselves, as well as other sources of institutional policy, have promulgated a number of new policies and practices specifically tailored to the questions and challenges raised by immigrant applications. These deal with three broad types of issues: resident status, language proficiency, and transcript reviews.

---

tion for their children. Thus, there is some active outreach to immigrant communities ongoing among postsecondary institutions, but this is the exception, not the rule.

[4]Of the four institutions that had implemented such activities, two were disappointed in the turnout and did not plan to repeat the program; the other two were pleased with parent participation, but both institutions were uncertain about funding for future programs for parents.

Resident Status. Residency requirements raise the question of how to treat immigrant applicants who meet length-of-stay requirements but who do not have permanent resident status, typically those who are undocumented or have applied for but not yet received asylum.

Policies regarding nonpermanent residents were first established at the institutional level, based on institutional interpretations of their charter and responsibilities. Institutional policies, however, have been challenged in the courts in several states, and institutional discretion is giving way to judicial or statutory mandate.[5] Across our study sites, both California and Illinois have ruled on the issue of fees for nonpermanent residents with mixed results.

During data collection for this study, nonpermanent residents were ineligible for in-state tuition within parts of the public higher education systems in California, Florida, New York, and New Jersey. However, we observed considerable within-state variation. For example, the City University of New York (CUNY) system and the California State University system both considered undocumented students residents and therefore eligible for in-state tuition and fees, while the State University of New York (SUNY) system and the University of California and California community college systems did not and charged out-of-state fees to undocumented students. Similarly, some colleges and universities in Florida considered students who had applied for but not received asylum in-state residents and those with no documentation out-of-state residents.[6] Of the 13 public institutions visited for this study, 7 permitted nonpermanent residents to qualify for state residency, and 6 did not.[7]

The salience of nonpermanent residence as an issue varies considerably across states. Among the regions included in this study, South Florida has relatively large numbers of individuals who have applied

---

[5]Proposition 187 in California, for example, prohibits public institutions from accepting undocumented students. (The proposition is undergoing judicial review at this time.)

[6]Our investigation covered only the five regions in which case studies were conducted.

[7]Since data collection, two California institutions in our sample no longer permit undocumented students to qualify for in-state tuition and fees, even if they meet all other requirements for state residency.

for asylum and California can be presumed to have the largest share of undocumented individuals although, in both cases, the absolute number eligible for postsecondary education may not be large.[8]

Enforcement of policies requiring nonpermanent residents to pay out-of-state fees was erratic within and across institutions. Within each college that we visited, there were significant differences in the levels of effort among staff spent on validating the information students provided about residency. Some staff approached this task as investigators enforcing rules vigorously; others as student advocates avoiding questions or simply ignoring formal policy. Although variation in implementation characterized most of the institutions we visited, there were exceptions. Respondents within two community colleges, for example, showed a high degree of agreement within their respective colleges about institutional policies and appeared consistent in their practices.

Across institutions, staff in California were most likely to assume the role of student advocates—one of the three California institutions that officially considered nonpermanent residents to be nonresidents implemented a de facto "don't ask, don't tell" policy, asking students to provide only very limited residency information. All offered informal counseling and assistance to undocumented students via a grassroots network of concerned faculty and staff. This support arguably reflects the growing representation of Hispanics (the group most affected by the policy) in higher education and public administration. The strictest enforcement was observed in northeastern institutions; the admissions director in one doctoral-granting university, for example, advised undocumented students to obtain a foreign student visa before their applications could be processed. In addition, respondents within all five community colleges were more likely to act as advocates for undocumented students than were respondents with four-year schools, who showed greater diversity in values and actions. This attitude reflects the community-based mission of the community colleges.[9]

---

[8]Of the estimated 3.4 million undocumented individuals residing in the United States as of 1992, 1.4 million, or 43 percent, resided in California. New York had 449,000, Florida had 322,000, and New Jersey had 186,000 (Warren, 1994).

[9]Fee policies for undocumented students also had some unanticipated effects within some institutions that left administrators scrambling for an appropriate response.

The actual number of students affected by policies related to nonpermanent residents is unknown. None of the institutions tracked applications or enrollments of nonpermanent resident students. Admissions directors at all the four-year institutions estimated that relatively few applications were received from nonpermanent residents (and especially few by undocumented individuals)—the admissions director at one East Coast doctoral-granting institution estimated that no more than a half dozen undocumented students per year submitted applications, while one West Coast admissions director estimated the number as over 100. The multicampus California State University system, which at the time of this study considered nonpermanent residents eligible for state residency, estimated that only 500 of its 360,000 students (or less than 1 percent) were undocumented in 1992 (Senate Office of Research, 1993). The California community colleges estimated that roughly 14,000 out of 1.5 million students were undocumented, although they lacked data about citizenship status for over 40,000 students (Senate Office of Research, 1993; Merl, 1992).

Language Proficiency. Verification of language competency is the second area that commands particular attention. Standardized tests are required for admission to all the four-year institutions included in this study and, indeed, to most four-year institutions nationally. In addition, students for whom English is a second language may be encouraged or required to take the Test of English as a Foreign Language (TOEFL) as a condition of admission to four-year institutions.

As shown in Table 3.1, five of the nine four-year institutions in our sample required at least some immigrant students to take the TOEFL for admission. However, policies governing use of TOEFL scores vary, and the more selective schools did not necessarily have the more selective TOEFL criteria. One doctoral-granting university in the sample, for example, required students who had been in the United States for two years or less to earn at least a 480 on the TOEFL

Specifically, a growing number of foreign students attending some East Coast colleges with J-1 or F-1 visas were letting their visas lapse, so that they could attend college as undocumented students and pay lower, in-state tuition. Staff serving international students pointed out to these students the substantial disadvantages of becoming undocumented, but the immediate financial relief this step offered often outweighed the longer-term problems that could ensue.

Table 3.1

Testing Policies for Immigrants

	TOEFL Required	No TOEFL Requirements
Community colleges (N=5)	0	5
Masters-granting universities (N=4)	3	1
Doctoral-granting universities (N=5)	2	3

in order to be eligible for admission. In contrast, a less selective masters-granting university required students who had been in the United States for three years or less to earn at least a 510 on the TOEFL. Other schools did not require the TOEFL at all, although all recommended that limited-English-proficiency students submit their scores. Thus, in practice the TOEFL served partly to screen out students who were unlikely to succeed and partly to enable immigrants, who might have low verbal scores on other standardized tests, to demonstrate their capacity for postsecondary work.

In contrast, none of the community colleges studied required the TOEFL or other standardized admissions tests, although they did require students to demonstrate English proficiency or pass an English placement test before they could enter programs for credit.

The TOEFL was designed for foreign students interested in studying in the United States. The Educational Testing Service (ETS) now offers other tests designed to assist in evaluating ESL students who attended high school in the United States.[10] However, only one institution in our study was aware of and planning to use these tests.

Transcript Reviews. For purposes of admissions decisions, institutions do not distinguish between native-born students and immigrants, provided the immigrants are permanent residents and have completed all secondary schooling in the United States. But applicants with secondary or postsecondary schooling outside the United States must be reviewed separately to determine if they have met admissions requirements and are eligible for transfer credit.

---

[10]ETS specifically suggests that its English language proficiency test be used to aid in admissions decisions and to place students in courses.

Most colleges and universities have established special procedures for reviewing transcripts of students who have had some secondary and/or postsecondary schooling outside the United States. Although these students constitute a minority of immigrant applicants, respondents report that their numbers are growing. None of the schools we visited could provide precise statistics about the number of applicants submitting foreign transcripts, but 10 of the 14 believed the number of such applicants had increased over the past five years. At least three schools had hired new staff or reassigned existing staff to this function.[11]

The process of reviewing foreign transcripts is time consuming and complex. Because schools need to verify that documentation is not forged, most require students to provide the original transcript. Some immigrant students have difficulty complying with this requirement, particularly those from countries that have experienced war or political upheaval. In principle, students who cannot provide original transcripts must either pass the General Educational Development (GED) exam or complete precollege work at a community college; in practice, schools try to accommodate these students. For example, one community college enabled students who could not produce a foreign transcript to complete a questionnaire about their past educational experience. Other schools dealt with such applications on a case-by-case basis, sometimes accepting copies of transcripts in lieu of the original, and sometimes permitting students to enroll after a good faith effort to obtain the transcript failed.

---

[11]Institutional data indirectly support the contention that foreign transcript reviews are increasing. These data show increased enrollment of immigrants in undergraduate education. Although we do not know what proportion of immigrant applications involved foreign transcript reviews, the increased number of immigrants participating in higher education certainly increases the likelihood of an increased number of foreign transcript reviews. For example, four out of five institutions that provided some trend data for this study experienced substantial increases in immigrant student enrollments between the mid-1980s and early 1990s. Three schools (one community college, one masters-granting university, and one doctoral-granting university) reported increases of 40 to 50 percent during this time period. Another masters-granting university showed a slight decline in the number of incoming freshmen who were permanent residents between 1989 and 1993, but a 64 percent increase in the number of new transfer students who were permanent residents.

After transcripts are received, institutions must then evaluate them to determine if the students are eligible for admission and/or transfer credit. Ten schools studied conducted this evaluation internally; of these, most relied upon staff specialists but two relied upon volunteer assistance, particularly foreign faculty. The other four schools used private nonprofit transcript review services. Three of these required students to pay for the transcript review (typically between $100 and $200 per review) and one used institutional funds.

Implementation of policies and procedures governing use of foreign transcripts was unsystematic and contentious. Practices varied across schools—immigrants denied admission or transfer credits at some schools gained admission or transfer credits at other schools with the same formal policies. Although professional associations publish guides for interpreting foreign transcripts, staff acknowledged that the process was at least partly subjective—one respondent described it as "more art than science."

It is not surprising, then, that the results of the transcript reviews were a frequent source of dissatisfaction. Across all schools visited, the most common complaint from students was that institutional transcript reviews were capricious and unfairly denied students credit for work completed out of the country. Faculty and academic counselors, however, complained that students were provided credit for materials that they had not mastered, leading to difficulty in more advanced courses. Dissatisfaction was highest within doctoral-granting universities and lowest within community colleges.[12]

The transcript review is a highly labor intensive process, and the time required to review foreign transcripts increases substantially if students appeal the admissions decisions. Despite the lack of systematic data across campuses, anecdotal evidence suggests that appeals

---

[12]Recognizing the widespread dissatisfaction with this process, a California State University systemwide task force recommended:

> In the CSU, there are only a limited number of resource books and individuals that interpret the complexities of foreign credits. . . . The CSU should facilitate the admissions process for immigrant students to ensure that they are awarded appropriate credit for college work completed in their countries of origin. (Asian Pacific American Education Advisory Committee, 1990, p. 10)

are common. One admissions counselor estimated that about one-third of transcript reviews were appealed; another reported spending close to 25 percent of work time reassessing foreign transcripts in response to student or faculty complaints. The appeals process further increased the admissions workload associated with increased immigration. Backlogs of transcripts had accumulated on at least two campuses, where students did not learn whether or not credits would be transferred until after they had completed one or more terms. Delays of this magnitude interfere with students' ability to plan a coherent and efficient course of study.

In sum, policies related to residency and transcript reviews are characterized by labor-intensive work and substantial diversity in implementation, both across and within schools. Policies related to tests vary across schools although implementation is relatively straightforward.

Financial Aid

Student aid comes from a variety of sources and, therefore, may be the object of differing policies and procedures. As noted above, the federal government provides three-quarters of all available student aid. About 19 percent comes from the institutions themselves and from private sources, and states provide about 6 percent of the total. Aid is awarded to about 6 million students per year (Davis, 1995).

Because aid money comes from a number of sources, institutions have substantial latitude in how they can allocate campus-based aid. Campus financial aid offices decide on the package of aid to be offered to each applicant, taking into account all the possible sources of aid available to that student. They are, thus, able to mix and match funds to enhance overall eligibility rates and rates for populations of special interest. At the same time, participating institutions must be careful to conform with all governmental requirements and regulations, and they are subject to periodic reviews and audits to ensure compliance.

Citizens and permanent residents are equally eligible for all forms of financial aid. The General Accounting Office estimates that about 10 percent of Pell Grant[13] recipients in 1992–93 were immigrants. Undocumented students and those who have applied for asylum or have temporary visas (including student visas) are ineligible for all forms of federal and most state financial aid. However, institutions with additional, independent sources of aid, for example money from endowments or private donations, can be somewhat flexible and may choose to support immigrants from these funds.

Typically, financial aid is intended to benefit participants in degree programs; only degree-granting institutions and students in for-credit programs within these institutions are eligible for financial aid. Thus, an immigrant student enrolled in remedial or ESL classes through a university's continuing education program or through a noncredit community college course is probably ineligible for most types of financial aid. However, students enrolled in essentially the same course as part of a degree or certificate program are likely to be eligible.[14] Similarly, federal regulations prohibit the award of financial aid to students who have prior baccalaureate degrees or the foreign equivalent.

Failure to maintain adequate records or failure to comply with federal and state policy may jeopardize an institution's continuing eligibility for financial aid. Thus, we found financial aid officers in all the schools we visited to be both knowledgeable about financial aid regulations and committed to complying with them. In accord with federal regulations, those who report themselves to be permanent residents must present documentation verifying their status. The financial aid office then forwards copies of their documentation to the INS, which informs the campuses of any "bad matches" between student documentation and INS records. The institution must address the discrepancies and provide follow-up documentation to INS, and financial aid cannot be awarded until such cases are re-

---

[13]Pell Grants are the largest source of federal gift aid, i.e., aid that does not have to be repaid.

[14]Despite policies that limit the number of remedial (noncredit) courses students can take before losing their eligibility for financial aid, the U.S. Department of Education does not consider ESL courses per se to be remedial, thereby removing a barrier to financial aid for immigrant college students who need substantial ESL instruction to complete their college studies. Thus, immigrants can obtain federal financial aid (Pell Grants) for ESL instruction, as long as they indicate an intention to obtain a college degree or postsecondary certificate.

solved. The number of bad matches reported to us ranged from fewer than a dozen to several thousand within one community college. In most cases, however, bad matches resulted from database errors and recent changes of status, not from false documents. Schools reported that, while cumbersome, the process had not yet resulted in serious delays, and the vast majority of "bad matches" were resolved fairly promptly in the applicant's favor.

Although schools take federal requirements seriously, our interviews suggest that office staff do not share a consistent view of their role when applying these requirements. Some acted as advocates for immigrant students, providing as much consultation and assistance as possible and requesting only the minimum amount of information for verification purposes. Others assumed more of an adversarial enforcement role, strictly interpreting policy where ambiguity existed.

Institutions differed in their access to and use of institutional funds for students who were otherwise ineligible for financial aid. On the one hand, four institutions in this study chose to allocate institutional aid to otherwise ineligible students, generally undocumented students or those who had applied for asylum. On the other hand, at least one institution had access to institutional financial aid but did not use students' ineligibility for other forms of financial aid as a criterion for awarding their own funds. Most institutions, however, simply lacked institutional financial aid and were, instead, completely dependent on federal, state, and sometimes systemwide aid programs.

Residency requirements are perhaps the most visible and controversial of the rules governing eligibility for financial aid. However, other requirements also have the potential to impose serious barriers for immigrant applicants. In the areas of financial aid, institutions and staff interpret and act on requirements diversely, but often in the immigrant students' favor.

In the face of federal restrictions on aid for students enrolled in noncredit courses, institutions generally tried to structure programs to promote immigrant eligibility for aid. Three out of the five community colleges studied offered low-level ESL courses as part of the institution's credit (academic) program, partly to enable students to obtain Pell Grants.[15] Further, recognizing that students can lose their eligibility for financial aid if they enroll in large numbers of noncredit courses, faculty on some campuses tried to limit prerequisites or provide at least some credit for remedial course work.

Responses about immigrant students who had attended postsecondary schools outside the United States provide an example of diversity in implementation choices. A financial aid director in one community college, concerned that a substantial number of Russian immigrant applicants had already earned college degrees in their country of origin, asked these applicants for financial aid to sign a statement swearing that they did not have an advanced degree. (An administrator later discontinued the practice because it was perceived as singling out a group for special treatment.) Conversely, a financial aid director in another state contended that college degrees from institutions in Russia were not equivalent to baccalaureate degrees in the United Sates in terms of either academic content or value in the labor market and therefore was willing to award financial aid to some Russian immigrants who had attended postsecondary school in their country of origin.[16]

Few financial aid directors interviewed for this study had special programs or procedures for serving immigrant students, despite the fact that applications from immigrants often raise special issues. Rather, staff were generally expected to serve all students equally regardless of their special needs or circumstances.

Most institutions did, however, try to take some steps to improve communications with immigrants, primarily by hiring bilingual staff. Since the institutions visited were located in areas with high concentrations of immigrants, this was easily accomplished. One university had established a special program through which a diverse group of students from a variety of cultural and linguistic backgrounds were

---

[15]There are other rationales for these curricular choices, as well. Colleges received larger full-time-equivalent reimbursements from the state for student enrollments in credit than noncredit courses. Also, ESL instructors often argue that ESL courses are analogous to foreign language courses and thus should provide credit toward graduation.

[16]Institutional procedures for assessing immigrants' educational history also varied— some financial aid offices conducted these reviews internally while others accepted the judgments of admissions offices or other units on the campus.

hired to serve as part-time financial aid outreach counselors in local high schools with high enrollments of immigrants.

PERCEIVED NEED FOR TARGETED PROGRAMS AND POLICIES

One obvious explanation for the limited, ad hoc responses to the growing immigrant applicant pool relates to perceptions regarding the special needs of this group. Our interviews indicated that while respondents believe immigrants are indeed a disadvantaged group with respect to some requirements for gaining entry to higher education, they are strongly advantaged with respect to others. Many respondents observed that expected barriers to immigrant student access were largely mitigated by immigrants' strong motivation to obtain a higher education, by their participation in informal informational networks, and by the fact that traditional outreach and financial aid programs reach immigrants as well as native-born students.[17]

Outreach and Admissions

Informal networks within immigrant communities were seen as providing immigrant students with help in accessing postsecondary education. Several respondents within a community college described an incident in which a college administrator, on a visit to Russia, discovered that residents of Kiev knew about this institution. Strong word of mouth within immigrant communities was perceived to raise awareness of local college opportunities and to provide information, tangible assistance (e.g., help filling out forms), and social support for students seeking a higher education.

Respondents noted that the effectiveness of informal networks was further bolstered by existing institutional outreach and recruitment activities, which encompassed immigrants even though they were not designed for or specifically targeted toward them. For example, as feeder high schools experience increased enrollment of immi-

---

[17]The demographic analyses conducted as part of this research confirm our respondents' perceptions. See Vernez and Abrahamse (1996).

grants, colleges will reach immigrant students simply by continuing their established outreach routines. Further, many immigrants are eligible for outreach programs for low-income, disadvantaged, and underrepresented populations.

As a result of these strong networks and broad access to outreach services, most respondents perceived that immigrants participated in higher education at high levels. Although respondents did not know the exact number or percentage of immigrants in their undergraduate student body, casual observation suggested to them that immigrant access was not a problem and that outreach services did not need major revision or enhancement to better serve immigrants.

Because the case studies focused on schools with high immigrant enrollments, it is not surprising that outreach was not perceived as a need. This might not be the case in schools with lower participation of immigrants.

Financial Aid

Respondents on most campuses believed that higher proportions of immigrants, compared with native-born students, needed financial assistance to attend college. Nonetheless, respondents did not perceive immigrants to be needier than other disadvantaged populations, particularly African Americans and Hispanics. Some respondents suggested that immigrants needed special assistance to manage the complex financial aid process. Among the barriers immigrants were perceived to face, for example, were parental reluctance to disclose their financial status, difficulty understanding application forms and procedures, misleading information from peers or community members, and difficulty providing needed documentation (e.g., when a student's parents lived in the country of origin). Further, the delays in processing financial aid applications due to verification procedures sometimes were seen as creating hardships for students, who had to wait longer than others to obtain financial support.

More commonly, however, immigrants were seen as better at managing the financial aid system than many native-born students. Informal networks within some immigrant communities provided information and assistance to immigrant students. Moreover, immigrants from some cultures were described as conscientious, attentive to detail, and aggressive—all traits that were seen as useful in obtaining financial aid.

Illustrating the strength of immigrant motivation and informational networks, some financial aid offices reported that immigrants tended to appear in disquietingly large numbers at the opening of their "first come, first served" application process. Other student groups appeared to resent this assertiveness. However, the schools were reluctant to change the "first come, first served" policies because they did not know of alternatives that were both feasible and fair. Therefore, they tried, instead, to "even out the competition" by convincing *all* students to apply early. Some also moved to appointment systems to reduce lines.

PERCEIVED APPROPRIATENESS OF TARGETED PROGRAMS

A second explanation for the limited, *ad hoc* responses of colleges and universities to increased immigration relates to their concern that a special, targeted response is inappropriate. Since they are under no mandate to serve immigrants and face little pressure from community members or policymakers to improve immigrant access, much is likely to depend on individual attitudes within institutions.

Problems Common to Many Groups

Many respondents, particularly higher-level administrators faced with the need to allocate limited resources among competing demands, questioned the appropriateness of specialized access programs for immigrants. They argued that although immigrants might face barriers to access, these barriers are not unique to immigrants but rather characterize a broad range of native-born students, including low-income students and those from historically underrepresented ethnic groups. Confusion about admissions and financial aid policies, for example, is frequently cited as a deterrent to college enrollment for minority students from inner-city schools (Hart and Jacobi, 1992). Similarly, although lack of English language skills may pose a special obstacle to immigrant access, many native-born students also have poor language skills and consequent difficulty understanding requirements and financial aid forms.

Ambiguous Institutional Responsibility

Respondents also reported diverse attitudes as well as significant ambivalence regarding the institution's responsibility for ensuring access for immigrants. Concerns centered on three main issues:

- Whether the institution has a special obligation to facilitate access for a population that recently arrived in the United States.

- Perceived trade-offs between services to immigrants and services to disadvantaged native-born applicants.

- The state of "college readiness" that should be required of successful applicants.

A number of respondents did not think schools should be responsible for ensuring "instant access" to higher education for newcomers. A subset of this group suggested that the ability to manage institutional admissions processes without special assistance was a good and appropriate test of immigrants' readiness for American higher education. At the same time, roughly an equal number argued that access to college is a critical precursor for successful economic assimilation and that immigrants should be given targeted support on the basis of a societal cost/benefit calculation.

Despite the perceived benefits of college access for immigrants, few institutions were prepared to divert resources into targeted outreach services to immigrants. Staff and faculty within only two institutions (both universities) displayed broad agreement that more outreach to immigrants was both needed and appropriate for the institution to undertake. Another five institutions (diverse in location and type) showed divided opinions on the issue of targeted outreach to immigrants. The remaining seven institutions did not support targeted outreach to immigrants, either because administrators believed that existing services were sufficient (N=4 schools) or because they believed that ethnic minority students (including but not limited to immigrants) were the highest priority target audience for institutional outreach (N=3 schools).

Respondents based their opinions regarding immigrant students on diverse biases. When asked about the desirability of increased outreach services to immigrants, for example, some respondents were quick to note that ethnic minority students had equal or greater needs for such services. Outreach professionals and other respondents on six campuses visited expressed concern that immigrants were, in fact, already displacing disadvantaged native-born students in special programs designed to promote access. They viewed targeted outreach for immigrants under these conditions as not only unnecessary but potentially damaging to the institution and to their communities. However, most community college respondents and about half of the respondents from other institutions advocated liberal access policies for students who are undocumented, out of status, or waiting for an asylum hearing. These respondents argued that such students will remain permanently in the United States regardless of their legal status. A higher education would enable them to become more productive members of society: Denying them access is consigning them to a permanent underclass. Conversely, other respondents pointed out that the capacity of the nation's higher education and financial aid systems is limited. These respondents believed that citizens will certainly be disadvantaged if subsidies and financial assistance are spread more widely.

Diverse admissions policies also reflect the lack of consensus regarding how institutions should balance access against goals for retention and achievement. Admissions staff in schools that required TOEFL scores (N=5) argued that their institutions should not admit students who are unlikely to succeed, especially when the institutions cannot offer adequate ESL support. In fact, at least three of these schools had considered increasing the minimum required TOEFL score within the past two years. Respondents within schools with looser requirements, however, stated that giving students a chance to succeed was more important than protecting them (and their institutions) from failure. At the same time, some in this group also questioned whether such tests were in fact predictive of student success within their particular institutions.

OTHER CONSTRAINTS

Although perceptions of need and appropriateness are major determinants of institutional response to the pressures of growing immigration, there may also be several more practical constraints.

These include resources, staff and organizational capacity, and clarity of externally determined policies.

Resources

Resource limitations appear to play a mixed role in shaping institutional responses to immigration. Most respondents assigned a low priority to such activities regardless of resources. At the same time, campuses were acutely aware of the resource limitations they faced and recognized that increased services to immigrants would probably mean reduced services to native-born students. This was particularly evident with regard to financial aid and the allocation of slots in equal opportunity, student affirmative action, and other such special programs.

Staffing and Infrastructure

Most had limited language and cultural resources within their admissions, financial aid, and outreach offices, curtailing their ability to handle growing immigrant-related workloads and to effectively mount even inexpensive programs.

For example, the process of reviewing transcripts is labor-intensive and demands a particular expertise. Existing procedures for review have been developed in response to a relatively small and predictable number of applicants with foreign transcripts. As the number of such applicants has grown, ad hoc review processes have become strained. The schools that we studied had difficulty finding the expertise and seemed uninterested in reforming the process to gain greater efficiency. About two-thirds of these schools reviewed transcripts internally. They typically depended on one or two trained staff members or a small cadre of volunteers, generally foreign-born faculty. Although most of the professional reviewers tried to stay current with the literature and consulted with off-campus colleagues in difficult cases, their supervisors were essentially unable to evaluate their work, and some administrators expressed concerns about quality control. Institutions that relied on faculty or other volunteers to share their subjective impressions of the quality of schools and academic programs that applicants attended in foreign countries experienced severe quality control problems.

One-third of the schools visited relied primarily upon outside non-profit agencies that offer transcript evaluation services. They valued these agencies for their systematic approach and breadth of knowledge, but others found them expensive and unable to customize their reports to a particular institutional curriculum.[18] However, few institutions, including those who turn regularly to the outside agencies, have systematically compared the costs and assessed the trade-offs involved in maintaining their current procedures versus outsourcing this function to nonprofit agencies offering this service; nor did any respondents report that schools had considered developing a common, jointly funded source of review.

Unclear Policies

Yet another factor that contributes to the diverse responses we observed is the complexity in the regulations that govern treatment of immigrants. We discovered clear evidence of confusion among staff about how residency, tuition, and financial aid regulations and policies should be implemented. It was not uncommon for different respondents within the same institution to give different descriptions of institutional policies. Furthermore, respondents were often unaware of or misinformed about the policies of other public institutions in their state, including those with which they had articulation agreements.

Even when policies and regulations are clear to administrators and department heads, information may not be clearly communicated to staff who provide direct services to students. For example, one financial aid director only accidentally discovered that staff were mistakenly denying financial aid to some immigrants whose secondary school diplomas included the word "baccalaureate." Staff turnover and the dispersion of counseling across a number of units greatly

---

[18]In fact, the cost of external transcript reviews (typically under $200) would almost certainly be lower than the costs of internal reviews if the external reviews reduce the likelihood of appeals and if the institution does not have to re-review the transcript to make specific decisions about course placements. Most staff did not accept either of these assumptions; moreover, they perceived staff time as a fixed cost for the institution and thus did not want either the institution or the students to assume the "extra" cost of using an outside vendor.

increased the difficulty of keeping staff and faculty informed about institutional policies.

SUMMARY

Few of the interview respondents in this study believed that increased immigration raised significant new access issues. Most of these institutions already enrolled large numbers of immigrants. Even among institutions with lower immigrant enrollments, administrators had little indication of widespread barriers to access and spent little time focusing on immigration. Nonetheless, we found that campuses face a number of unresolved issues and potential problems related to increased immigration.

First, increased immigration often means increased workloads for outreach, admissions, and financial aid offices at a time when new fiscal resources are increasingly scarce. Increased participation of immigrants strains access services. Established procedures may be unable to meet student demand for services without new staff—if such resources are not forthcoming as a result of fiscal constraints, institutions may need to improve productivity and efficiency, or observe a reduction in the quality and responsiveness of access services.

Second, increased immigration raises questions about institutional responsibility for specific subgroups of immigrants who may face obstacles to college enrollment greater than those encountered by most other immigrants. For example, policies related to students who are not permanent residents reveal the different values held by state and federal policymakers on the one hand and educational practitioners who want to help *all* motivated students gain access to college on the other.

Third, increased immigration forces higher education policymakers to consider how—or whether—to trade-off services to immigrants with those to native-born individuals. The possibility that immigrants are displacing native-born students from programs designed for "disadvantaged" students and growing competition among all students for a shrinking pool of financial aid raise new, and largely unresolved, questions about whether higher education should be blind to citizenship status in the delivery of access services.

Chapter Four

ACADEMIC SUPPORT AND RETENTION

Access to higher education provides newcomers to America with the opportunity to gain skills they need to participate successfully in the labor force and achieve economic assimilation. However, access alone is not sufficient; students must stay the course, completing their degrees *and* acquiring skills that will provide them with job opportunities after college.

ACADEMIC SUPPORT: ISSUES AND STRATEGIES

Opening the doors of higher education to a larger, more diverse group of students raises important questions: whether and how to ensure that these students are successful and what academic standards should be maintained. Efforts to extend access typically result in the admission of less well prepared groups of students. Schools then face difficult trade-offs. If they intend to maintain academic standards, they must invest, perhaps heavily, in remedial programs to better prepare these enrollees or they must be prepared to deny a large number of students the degrees for which these students have studied. However, schools might decide that the academic standards that predated their efforts to expand access were unnecessarily stringent or even misguided and that to change them is not necessarily to lower them. The choices are hard ones and likely to engender heated debate.

In the postwar period, colleges and universities have manifested a growing sense of responsibility for the ultimate success of their students. Most institutional policies now reflect the belief that responsibility for improving access should go hand in hand with responsibility for ensuring academic success.

Now these same schools find themselves facing charges that their efforts to improve access and retention may be contributing to what many believe to be declining academic standards. In response to pressures from both legislatures and the business community, colleges have begun to reexamine their curricula and graduation standards with the goal of strengthening the quality of undergraduate education. Moreover, growing fiscal pressures sharpen the trade-offs facing educational leaders and are contributing to a reconsideration of institutional responsibilities.

Institutions have pursued a variety of strategies in response to the twin concerns of retention and academic standards. These include the provision of remedial academic programs as well as academic support services and assessment testing.[1]

Remediation

Today, about 90 percent of all colleges offer some remedial programs or courses (NCES, 1991). Both the community colleges and universities in our study offered extensive arrays of remedial courses. The effectiveness of these programs and courses, however, is unknown for the most part.

Academic Support Programs

Institutions offer a growing range of academic support services intended to promote student academic success. Once enrolled in courses, students may usually select from a wide array of services currently available on most college campuses, including tutorial assistance, academic guidance and counseling, and learning-skills instruction.

As testament to the remarkable range of opportunities, one comprehensive university in our sample supported a tutorial assistance of-

---

[1]Schools also turn to nonacademic support services as a mechanism for improving retention. These are discussed in Chapter Six.

fice, a writing laboratory, a computer laboratory, an academic counseling unit, and a learning-skills center. In addition, this campus offered a variety of programs serving distinct student subgroups, including a summer "bridge" program for educationally disadvantaged students, an equal opportunity program serving primarily low income students, a student affirmative action program for students from historically underrepresented ethnic groups, a Minority Engineering and Science Achievement (MESA) program, a Minority Engineering Program (MEP), and a Puente Project serving primarily Chicano students.

Assessment Testing

At the same time, institutions are now responding to pressure to assess student outcomes. Of the 14 institutions in this study, over half required students to pass some examination to graduate (see Table 4.1), although their specific requirements were quite diverse. Requirements ranged from a reading examination for associate of arts degree recipients to a comprehensive exam for graduation from all Florida institutions.

Immigrants as a Target Population

Many observers expect immigrant students to face special difficulties achieving academic success in college (Romero, 1991; Scarpaci and Fradd, 1985; Sue and Zane, 1985). Foremost among the challenges they face is language. Even those immigrants who achieved high levels of success in secondary school might well encounter difficulty

Table 4.1

Assessment Requirements

	Community Colleges	Masters-Granting Universities	Doctoral-Granting Universities
Competency test required for graduation or matriculation	3	4	1
No competency test required	2	0	4

meeting the higher collegiate demands for reading and writing, as well as for understanding the more complex and abstract classroom discussions. Language deficiency will also impair performance on competency tests.

Immigrants are also likely to face conflicts between academic demands and cultural norms and expectations. Many immigrant students are from low-income families and need to balance work and other family obligations with school. They may be unfamiliar or uncomfortable with the approach of American higher education institutions; for example, they may have been raised in the educational tradition of memorizing facts and fail to respond to faculty expectations that they participate in class and engage in critical analysis. Similarly, students who are not accustomed to service-oriented schools may be reluctant to avail themselves of the special programs and opportunities these institutions provide.

Institutions, then, must decide whether or not these possible obstacles present significant barriers and whether the institutions should take responsibility for mitigation.

INSTITUTIONAL RESPONSES TO IMMIGRATION

Case studies of 14 institutions with high, or increasing, enrollments of immigrants revealed that all these institutions have special policies and programs for ESL. These policies are discussed in the following chapter. Beyond ESL, however, none of the institutions we studied formally differentiated immigrants from other students in the delivery of undergraduate education or academic support services.

The Faculty Perspective

Because faculty function with a high level of autonomy and independence, their perceptions and behaviors are essential to an understanding of how institutions respond to immigration.[2] Across all

---

[2]Our case studies included 46 interviews with faculty, including 21 academic administrators, 5 faculty senate chairs, 16 line faculty (most of whom taught in departments serving large numbers of immigrants), and 4 staff (e.g., multicultural center directors

campuses studied, faculty cautioned that they had no way to identify immigrant students other than by students' self-reports (e.g., in class discussion or essays) or by foreign accents. At the same time, individual faculty members shared some concerns related to the instruction of students presumed to be immigrants. These issues include language barriers faced by immigrants, cultural differences in approaches to undergraduate education, the tendency of immigrants to gravitate toward certain specific majors, and different standards of academic honesty.

Language Barriers. By far the most widespread concern about immigrants was that language difficulties increased the difficulties of achieving undergraduate success. The manner in which faculty responded to immigrants with language problems, however, varied considerably.

Case study respondents within three institutions, primarily those that lacked a tradition of serving immigrant students, shared anecdotes about faculty members who tried to screen out students with limited English skills. For example, a professor in one California community college administered a "safety test" to students enrolled in his laboratory course, expressing the concern that students who did not understand instructions might jeopardize the safety of science laboratories. In response to a student grievance, this practice was discontinued when the "safety test" was found to actually be an English test. The professor was counseled by administration to provide demonstrations and written materials to supplement his verbal instructions. Other faculty were reported to introduce their courses by explaining that students with limited English skills might find the work difficult, a practice criticized by some colleagues as another way of screening out immigrants by inviting them to drop the course.

For the most part, however, faculty worked diligently to circumvent the language problems of immigrant students. Although those we interviewed reported widely disparate approaches to grading written assignments by *all* students, approaches ranged from ignoring errors in English language usage altogether to penalizing students for such errors regardless of the content of the written assignment. The typi-

---

or institutional researchers) who also held faculty appointments. (ESL faculty are considered in the next chapter.)

cal response, however, was mild efforts to correct English language errors. Few professors outside of English and ESL departments reduced students' grades for errors in English, an approach applied both to immigrants and native-born students.

Accommodating Diverse Cultural Norms. One or more faculty respondents at each campus (often those in the social sciences or in education) suggested that immigrant students are likely to have different learning styles and different norms regarding appropriate academic behavior, including contact with faculty outside of the classroom and participation in study groups. About half the faculty respondents (and a slightly higher percentage of academic support staff) suggested that faculty *should* modify their teaching practices as necessary to help immigrant students.

However, we found little evidence that faculty were, in fact, adjusting their teaching styles or practices in response to the continuing increase in immigration. This was a source of contention on some campuses. One faculty member in a department of education who specialized in bilingual studies complained that most faculty "believe they teach subjects not students," and other respondents pointed out that faculty believe "students should adjust to them, not vice versa."

Academic Honesty. Under the broader heading of conflicting norms and expectations, there is the perception on campuses that immigrant students bring different standards of academic integrity to the classroom. A handful of faculty respondents did identify academic honesty as a particular problem area. They reported that many immigrants come from environments where different standards govern the independent completion of assignments and plagiarism and that these students are more likely to violate American standards of academic honesty. Faculty with heightened concerns typically clarified expectations at the beginning of their course as a preventive measure. However, the vast majority of respondents thought this issue had been overblown as part of generalized anti-immigrant sentiments.

Institutional Responses: Policies and Practices

Assessment Testing. Despite some vocal opposition, all the institutions we visited used testing to assess the skills of incoming students and to inform course placement decisions. In roughly half the schools visited, reliance on placement tests for remedial and ESL referrals was increasing as a result of faculty concern about high numbers of underprepared students in their classrooms.

The continuing increase in immigration also adds a new dimension to ongoing campus debates about outcomes assessment. Some institutions have responded to rising concern over students' abilities by requiring students to pass competency tests as a condition of graduation. This response has, in turn, provoked opposition among those who believe that such tests unfairly penalize immigrants or give an unduly gloomy portrait of institutional outcomes for schools that serve large numbers of immigrants. Although it did not cause the implementation of outcome assessments, immigration has added new questions about the purposes and appropriate uses of assessment.

Choice of Majors. Respondents in all schools noted that immigrant students tended to cluster in a small set of majors. For example, respondents consistently reported that Asian immigrants tended to cluster in business and engineering programs, while Hispanic immigrants tended to cluster in the social sciences, nursing, and education.

This pattern concerned administrators and counselors from both academic and student affairs areas, who argued that immigrants prematurely narrowed their options. They also feared that Asian immigrants denied themselves an important opportunity to improve their English by selecting courses that minimized language skills.

However, none of the schools we visited had any coordinated response to this pattern other than informal counseling. In fact, many had expanded course offerings within the majors preferred by immigrants in response to student demand, implicitly reinforcing this pattern of choice. A number of faculty (notably those from science and engineering departments) and most of the immigrant students interviewed suggested that immigrant students' preferences offer the dual advantages of optimizing school performance and paving the way to stable and often highly remunerative careers. One academic counselor, for example, referred to the accounting major selected by many immigrant students within the institution as an "immediate ticket to the middle class."

Remediation and Academic Support Programs.[3] At least five institutions in our sample required students who failed to meet certain scores on placement tests or who obtained marginal grades to participate in various remedial and support programs. The remainder provided such services as options, not requirements. Of those requiring participation, some enforced the requirements and some did not.

Despite the proliferation of remedial and support programs, ESL courses constituted the only support we found that specifically targeted immigrant students. However, many other support programs target low-income, minority, and underrepresented students, and immigrants, therefore, usually qualify. Some, such as equal opportunity programs (EOPs), which offer academic and financial support to educationally and economically disadvantaged populations, attract large numbers of immigrant students. For example, criteria for participation in one community college EOP included (but were not limited to) having a high school grade point average under 2.5, failing to qualify for college level math or English courses, or previous enrollment in remedial courses—each of which could encompass immigrant students with English language difficulties.

However, support programs that target ethnic minorities posed special problems because of the diverse achievement levels within these groups. In some cases, institutions have themselves adjusted the qualifications for programs to better target groups they believe to be truly disadvantaged, inadvertently penalizing immigrants disproportionately. For example, respondents in a number of institutions we visited reported that Asians were excluded from support programs for minority students in math, engineering, and science courses. The brochure for one such program in a community college defined eligible students as "African American, Mexican American, Native American, Hispanic/Latino, and Puerto Rican," excluding Asians

---

[3]The rise in remedial courses has been documented in other analyses (e.g., National Center for Education Statistics, 1991). Remedial courses and academic support services not only assist students in their coursework but also prepare them for competency exams where required.

(who constituted a majority of the immigrant population on the campus).

The perceived exclusion of Asian immigrants from academic support programs was a source of controversy on every campus we visited that hosted such programs. Nonetheless, no schools reported they were considering dropping such programs, and two reported they were adding them. Despite added strains on intergroup relations, most believed these programs promoted the success of native-born underrepresented ethnic minority students, particularly in such fields as science and engineering.

PERCEIVED NEED FOR TARGETED PROGRAMS AND POLICIES

Most respondents did not view immigrant students as disadvantaged. In fact, they were usually thought to be better prepared for higher education than many native-born students. For example, respondents in East Coast schools believed that Caribbean immigrants, particularly those from Jamaica, were significantly better prepared for college than African Americans who had attended inner-city schools in the United States. Florida respondents repeatedly noted that Cuban immigrants were among the most successful students on the campus. Similarly, respondents in California felt that recent immigrants from Mexico or Latin America were better prepared and achieved at higher levels in college than did second generation or later Chicanos. On some campuses, Asian immigrants were perceived as much better students than native-born individuals. Respondents in two research universities noted that non-Asians were increasingly reluctant to attend the institution or major in certain fields because the Asian immigrants "drove up the curve" and increased the competition for high grades.

Immigrant success in higher education was generally viewed as a result of three factors: (1) relatively high levels of preparation, often in foreign schools believed to offer more rigorous education than U.S. public schools; (2) support from family and peers, including informal networks that offered help with studies and advice on college success; and (3) a strong work ethic and motivation to succeed in college. In contrast, native-born students, especially those from historically underrepresented ethnic groups, were depicted as poorly prepared, without strong familial support, and tethered to a peer culture that accords little value to academic achievement.

However, when pressed, respondents identified several areas of immigrant student need. Most important, of course, were communication skills. Respondents also noted that immigrants often experienced special difficulty with test-taking skills.

Language Competency

Respondents believed that immigrants' difficulty with both written and verbal English was the most serious and widespread obstacle to immigrants' retention and academic success. Thus, ESL programs (discussed in Chapter Five) stood as the predominant institutional response to the academic needs of immigrant students. Some respondents also suggested that immigrants who arrived in the United States between the ages of 8 and 12 generally lacked good language skills in both English and their native language and, therefore, were especially disadvantaged in reading, writing, and verbal communications.

Test-Taking Skills

Test-taking skills emerged as a second important deficit common to immigrants. Respondents within six institutions (primarily masters-granting universities and community colleges) argued that many immigrants were not familiar with common test formats, particularly multiple choice tests, and therefore their scores often failed to reflect their actual grasp of the material. Timed tests were perceived as exacerbating the difficulty of immigrants who had limited English proficiency. These problems with testing were seen as unfairly depressing immigrants' grades and posing barriers to graduation in schools that required competency testing for matriculation or graduation.

Cultural and Familial Barriers

Respondents also mentioned other common barriers to immigrant academic success, although, for the most part, they believed these barriers were as prevalent in the nonimmigrant as in the immigrant population. They suggested that immigrants often experience academic difficulties due to role conflict as they try to balance work, family obligations, and school. In the classroom, they describe immigrants as less likely to understand that faculty often expect and grade on the basis of class participation, out-of-class consultation and discussion, and homework. Academic counselors and student affairs staff were most likely to cite these barriers, while faculty and academic administrators were more likely to stress the advantages that immigrants displayed in relation to native-born students.

Variation Among Subpopulations

Respondents indicated that variation among immigrant subpopulations in their institutions often made it difficult to develop coherent, useful programs for all immigrant students. For example, as noted above, many believed Asian immigrants were an advantaged group with respect to success in science. They identified other groups, for example Haitians in Florida and New York, Cambodians and Samoans in California, and Mexicans in Chicago, as markedly underprepared for college, even when compared with other immigrants.

PERCEIVED APPROPRIATENESS OF TARGETED PROGRAMS

Concerns regarding the appropriateness of targeting immigrants for special services tended to mirror those raised regarding special programs to promote access. Immigrants were not perceived as particularly disadvantaged and therefore should not be the target of special support.

Although in many cases respondents recognized characteristic barriers to immigrant academic achievement, they usually reported that these barriers were more common among other native-born groups, especially low-income and minority students. In the same vein, some respondents, particularly those at degree-granting universities, expressed frustration at their institution's general inattention to undergraduate education and faculty disinterest in improving the quality of instruction for *all* students, not only for immigrants.

The overlap between the needs of immigrants and other students and the perceived strengths of immigrants provide little reason for educational administrators or practitioners to devote scarce resources to improving immigrant student academic success. Further, many administrators were reluctant to develop services specifically for immigrants if such programs would reduce academic support resources for native-born students.

OTHER CONSTRAINTS

Respondents within four institutions also noted that their institutions had developed few academic support programs for immigrants because they found immigrant students reluctant to use the services that were offered. In addition to the stigma some students perceived to be attached to the use of such services, they had found immigrants to be highly goal oriented and eager to complete their degree in the most efficient way possible. These immigrants did not want to enroll in remedial courses or use other services that did not provide credit toward the bachelors degree. Immigrant students were also described as preferring to rely upon their network of peers rather than support staff for assistance and guidance. As a result, most institutions experienced little or no demand for specialized support services from immigrant students themselves.

Faculty also reported difficulty providing focused or specialized assistance to immigrant students in the classroom. Most of those staff interviewed reported that they lacked the skills and time needed to serve a limited-english-proficient population. At best, they might provide detailed edits of immigrant students' written work in combination with referrals to appropriate academic support units; at worst, they ignored immigrant students' difficulties altogether.

THE QUALITY TRADE-OFF

How institutions respond to the growing presence of immigrants will also be shaped by how faculty and administrators perceive their options and define institutional goals and responsibilities. Should colleges and universities see themselves as, first and foremost, guardians of a standard of academic excellence or as principally responsible for improving the life-chances of those who pass through?

Do the standards used to define academic excellence have some external validity or are they arbitrary barriers?

Few of our respondents suggested abandoning high standards, but we found strong disagreement on the validity of traditional measures of excellence. Nowhere was this disagreement more apparent than in debates over testing and appropriate language skill requirements. In general, faculty and academic administrators were significantly more likely than student services staff and administrators to advocate greater rigor and higher standards for students' written and verbal English skills. Even faculty, however, manifested substantial disagreement on this issue.

One camp of faculty seriously argued that weak English language skills should not depress grades or other measures of performance among students who appeared to master the course content. For example, a social sciences professor explained that he did not consider it appropriate to assign lower grades on essays and term papers to immigrants simply because they "write with an accent." Other faculty criticized timed "power tests" as well as competency tests, describing them as de facto immigrant screens, holding the critical baccalaureate degree out of reach even if these students meet all other graduation requirements.[4]

In sharp contrast, other faculty believed that institutions were delinquent if they failed to require appropriately demanding language skills. These faculty pointed out that not only should a U.S. baccalaureate degree imply a minimum level of English language competence, but also that it was improbable that students without a good grasp of English would be getting the full richness and texture of many of their courses; their achievement would be diminished. These respondents also suggested that schools are not doing any favors for immigrants in reducing expectations related to English language ability since employers assign a high value to verbal and written communication skills.

---

[4]For example, one faculty report recommends, "Scoring of essays should give due consideration to 'foreign accents' in writing. . . . Examination topics should be culturally neutral and completion time for the examination should be adequate" (Asian Pacific American Education Advisory Committee, 1990, p. 30).

Differences in opinion were strong and value-laden. In only one case did an institution explicitly attempt to develop a consensus or set of institutional policies that would pave the way for a coherent and unified approach to the tough trade-offs that underlay the diversity of opinion. Instead, individual faculty members were generally left to decide for themselves what requirements to apply. Institutional intervention was limited to situations that left the institution vulnerable to lawsuits and grievances, such as the use of invalid and unreliable tests to screen out immigrants.

SUMMARY

Case study participants viewed immigrants as among the most successful students in college and perceived little need for targeted support services beyond ESL courses. The growing participation of immigrants in higher education raises several thorny institutional issues, however, including responsibilities of institutions to admitted students, the meaning and value of the baccalaureate degree, and balancing responsibilities to diverse groups. For the most part, these issues are not unique to immigrants; rather, the presence of immigrants increases the salience of these unresolved issues.

Chapter Five

INSTRUCTION FOR ENGLISH AS A
SECOND LANGUAGE

An influx of immigrant students puts new demands on ESL services, including demands to serve increasing numbers of students and, often, demands to serve highly diverse student needs. When existing ESL resources cannot meet demand, or when students fail to obtain the ESL instruction they need, institutions face hard choices about whether to allocate more funds to ESL programs as opposed to other functions or support services and, if not, what types of requirements related to English language competency to impose on students. This chapter reviews how ESL programs are responding to the continuing increase in immigration and the challenges that increased immigration creates for ESL programs and, by extension, for institutions.

ESL: ISSUES AND STRATEGIES

College-level ESL instruction originally served the needs of foreign students and scholars temporarily in the United States. ESL courses continue to serve large numbers of international students, but today they also serve a growing immigrant population.

Organizational Structure

Within community colleges located in regions with large numbers of immigrants, ESL instruction is typically offered as a critical component of the college's service mission (Cohen and Brawer, 1989). The five community colleges visited for this study all had well-developed ESL programs. ESL instruction had the status of an academic department in three of the five community colleges visited; it was an autonomous quasi-academic department in another, and dominated the communications department in the fifth. All of the community colleges offered a range of ESL courses; four of the five colleges offered beginning through advanced courses, while the fifth offered only intermediate and advanced courses. All offered at least four levels of ESL instruction, and one offered 13 levels. All had at least some tenure and tenure-track ESL faculty, ranging from fewer than 10 to over 40 per campus; the number of supplemental part-time ESL instructors ranged from under 20 to over 100. As a result, each offered well over 12 different sections of ESL per academic quarter or semester. Finally, all of the community colleges in our sample offered ESL both for credit (and therefore for a fee) and for noncredit (and therefore for free or at a significantly reduced cost).

In contrast, ESL instruction within four-year institutions is more limited. The nine baccalaureate-granting schools in this study housed ESL courses in different units, including English departments, ethnic studies departments, learning centers, and continuing education/extension services. Further, ESL was often dispersed across different units within the same institution. In no case did we find a stand-alone ESL department in a four-year institution, and those teaching ESL courses were either nontenure track instructors or tenure-track faculty from other subject areas (e.g., English or linguistics). Relative to community colleges, ESL course offerings in four-year institutions were more limited, with fewer levels; among the four-year institutions we visited, the maximum was four levels. The number of ESL sections offered per semester was also relatively low, ranging from none to over 20. Seven of the nine universities studied provided elective credit for ESL, although generally for only one to three courses. At least seven four-year schools (including the two that did not offer academic credit for ESL instruction) offered noncredit ESL programs for a fee, through continuing education or extension services.

Table 5.1 describes the organization of ESL programs in the case study sites.

Placement Tests

One issue facing all colleges with regard to ESL is how to implement the ESL "gatekeeping" functions. In both the community colleges

Table 5.1

Organization of ESL Programs and Departments

	Community Colleges (N=5)	Masters-Granting Universities (N=4)	Doctoral-Granting Universities (N=5)
Extension services		2	3
Academic support		2	3
Part of an academic department	1	2	1
Stand-alone academic department	4		

NOTE: Columns add to more than the number of schools in this category because some schools had more than one ESL program.

and the four-year institutions we studied, undergraduate students were directed to ESL studies on the basis of placement tests, of direct referrals by counselors or professors, and, occasionally, of self-referrals. The case study institutions typically used multiple methods of assessment, including commercially available tests, interviews, and writing samples. About one-third had also developed their own placement or diagnostic instruments.

Enforcement

Schools in our study differed in the rigor used to enforce ESL referrals. At one extreme were four schools that enforced ESL referrals in the computerized registration system so that students directed to ESL could not register for other courses if they did not register for ESL. At the other extreme were four schools that did not require placement tests and/or did not require students to abide by the results of placement tests. In the middle were schools that counseled and recommended that students enroll in specific ESL courses but stopped short of requiring these courses. In addition, some schools with ESL requirements for students with limited English proficiency lacked any means of consistently enforcing their policies.

Immigrants as a Target Population

Because language is viewed as the largest barrier to immigrant students' academic success, ESL was perceived as the most important support service to provide to immigrants. Thus, ESL programs origi-nally designed for international students or small and homogeneous immigrant cohorts were being stretched to address the needs of growing and more diverse immigrant populations. Institutions, however, must decide to what extent they will take responsibility for mitigating the language barriers immigrants face.

INSTITUTIONAL RESPONSES TO IMMIGRATION

The demand for ESL exceeded the supply of courses within 10 of the 14 institutions visited. However, schools did not consistently re-spond to growing demand by increasing their ESL offerings.

Program Size

Nationwide, ESL programs grew dramatically between the 1970s and early 1990s. Only one-quarter (26 percent) of all community colleges offered ESL in 1975; by 1991, over 40 percent did so (Ignash, 1992). However, trends within the 14 institutions studied are less clear.

Actual growth in ESL offerings in response to immigration is difficult to determine because the number of sections of ESL courses fluctu-ate in response to teacher availability, budget, and expected class sizes. For example, schools may decide to offer fewer sections of ESL with more seats per section, or they may add new ESL courses but decrease class size so that the overall enrollment in ESL remains stable. Moreover, changes in ESL program size reflect multiple fac-tors including immigration, foreign student enrollments, curricular reform, and restructuring, and we cannot fully separate the effects of immigration from those of these other factors. Finally, there is no clear baseline against which to measure changes in program size following immigrant student influxes.

At least four institutions (one community college and three universi-ties) in our sample had increased the size of their ESL programs within the past two years by adding new courses. Another five insti-tutions, including some with rapidly growing immigrant enroll-ments, had cut back on ESL courses because of budget pressures. These included two community colleges and three universities. The remaining five institutions did not report significant change in the size of their ESL programs despite increased immigrant enrollments.

Because data collection took place during a time of severe budget cuts in many higher education institutions, one might like to know the degree to which ESL was cut in relation to other programs or services.[1] For example, if ESL sustained smaller cuts than other programs, one might conclude that administrators were trying to protect the program. Unfortunately, these kinds of comparative analyses are difficult or impossible to measure in many higher education institutions, and it is therefore not surprising that, even within the same institution, respondents disagreed about this issue (Benjamin et al., 1993). Some respondents reported that ESL was cut more readily than other programs and services; others within the same institution or system said that ESL was protected from cuts because of high student demand and the state funding generated by student enrollments in ESL.

Information about the number and proportion of immigrant students enrolling in ESL was also difficult to obtain. None of the institutions were able to provide unduplicated counts of the number of students enrolled in ESL courses, and raw counts of course enrollments are essentially uninterpretable because of the tendency of many students to enroll in multiple ESL courses simultaneously. In addition, none of the schools were able to separate immigrant undergraduates from other students taking ESL, including foreign students, visiting scholars, and graduate students. The small amount of data we did obtain, however, suggest that ESL enrollments may be leveling off. Consider the following for example:

- One community college showed growth in the number of incoming students whose placement test results indicated a need for ESL between 1988 and 1991, with declines in 1992 and 1993.

- A doctoral-granting university reported an increased number of freshmen enrolling in ESL courses through 1993–94, but a significant decline in 1994–95.

---

[1]The conflicting pressures facing higher education institutions are captured in a recent article in *The Chronicle of Higher Education* (Healy, 1995), which describes the manner in which budget cuts are threatening ESL programs.

- The number of new students in one doctoral-granting university whose test results indicated a need for ESL peaked in 1990–91 and dropped slightly in subsequent years.

Restructuring

Three of the five schools that had cut ESL had also restructured the program within the past five years.[2] One community college moved ESL out of English and created a free-standing ESL department. A masters-granting university moved ESL out of English and into extension services, thereby effectively moving ESL from a support service covered by student fees to a fee-for-service unit. Another research university, however, changed ESL from a quasi-autonomous support unit to a unit under the control of the English Department to provide greater academic oversight. Other, more modest reorganizations included shifts in the balance between noncredit and for-credit ESL courses at two community colleges.

Policies and Procedures

In response to faculty concerns about students with limited ability to write or communicate in English, one research university recently began accepting some students provisionally, mandating they attend ESL courses. Another community college president hoped to convince the college's board of the need for an ESL immersion program. For the most part, however, the colleges and universities in our study had not modified their policies in response to increased immigration.

No institutions reported changing their assessment and placement policies in direct response to the increasing participation of immigrants. Decisions about assessment tools and policies were generally left to ESL faculty and departments, with some institutional oversight to ensure that ESL tests, as well as other assessment tests, are reliable and valid. Moreover, institutional practices in enforcing placements were more a product of the characteristics of the institution's registration system than of institutional attitudes or values related to ESL.

---

[2]Restructuring further increased the difficulty of comparative analyses.

Faculty Responses

Tools and Tests. Within most of the ESL programs studied (especially those in California), faculty reported spending considerable time developing assessment and curricular materials. Commercially available assessment instruments were typically perceived as insufficient to guide decisionmaking about student placement in ESL courses. Similarly, despite a variety of commercially available curricular materials, these, too, were often described as unsuited to each institution's unique ESL program. Thus, faculty and instructional staff, often without much formal training or experience in assessment or curriculum development, developed their own placement, monitoring, and teaching tools. The result was a profusion of materials across campuses (including across campuses within the same system), with each campus having a different package of commercially available and "homegrown" tests and curricular materials.

Perceived Role of Program. Across all institutions visited, ESL instructors showed an unusual dedication to their students and often were advocates and informal counselors for immigrants (and foreign students) within their college or university. ESL faculty strongly rejected the suggestion that ESL was "remedial," arguing that ESL should be more fully integrated into the undergraduate curriculum. Not surprisingly, ESL instructors also argued for expanding ESL course offerings to accommodate an increasing need and demand.

Other faculty and staff, however, especially in four-year schools, viewed ESL as remedial in nature. Furthermore, non-ESL faculty and staff in every community college and in about half of the four-year institutions expressed concern that ESL could grow to overwhelm the institution and indicated a need for the institution to clarify and maintain the boundaries of the ESL program. At the same time, faculty experiencing difficulties in the classroom due to growing numbers of students with limited English proficiency often argued for adding ESL.

Marginalization of ESL Instructors. ESL instructors in over half the institutions visited felt that they had "second class status" within their college. Within four-year institutions, ESL instructors were uniformly nontenure track or occasionally "borrowed" from other departments and experienced the frustrations common to lecturers and adjunct faculty (Gappa, 1984). Even within community colleges, tenured ESL faculty noted that other faculty viewed ESL as "less academic" than other disciplines.

PERCEIVED NEED FOR ESL

Across the 14 institutions studied, respondents at 12 institutions agreed that a rising number of immigrant students did not have English skills sufficient to meet the demands of a rigorous college curriculum. Faculty and others in four-year institutions counted on the admissions process to screen out students with the lowest-level English skills. Nonetheless, respondents repeatedly pointed out that schools were admitting students who did not have the English skills needed to successfully complete a college-level curriculum, particularly in the social sciences and humanities. As faculty encountered growing numbers of students in their classes with limited English abilities, many called on the institution to provide more ESL.

Among the population of immigrant students, there is considerable heterogeneity in ESL needs. Respondents noted that the most disadvantaged were those who did not have the opportunity to develop strong language skills in either English or their native language, typically those who moved to the United States during the elementary or junior high school grades. In addition, individuals manifest different needs for assistance in speaking, reading, and writing.

Although ESL is primarily intended to prepare students for college-level course work in English, it also serves other needs. ESL instructors at visited sites sought to facilitate students' assimilation by designing lessons about American social and civic traditions. ESL also enabled immigrants to obtain peer support, and teachers often provided informal counseling and guidance. Similarly, ESL courses introduced immigrants to American higher education, including expectations regarding course participation, homework, and grading.

PERCEIVED APPROPRIATENESS OF EXPANDING ESL IN RESPONSE TO IMMIGRATION

Administrators in schools with growing immigrant populations face the choice of either increasing ESL and thereby serving the needs of immigrants or increasing other services that address the needs of native-born students. One staff member, for example, criticized his institution for expanding ESL sections for immigrants without concomitant increases in tutorial services for native-born minority students. Perceived competition between ESL and services for other groups was particularly pronounced in the four-year sector, where ESL was more likely to be organized as a support service than as an academic discipline. Even within community colleges, however, administrators noted that ESL served only one segment of the community and that the college needed to maintain its responsiveness to other groups.

Institutions' willingness to support ESL is a rough indicator of the degree to which institutions perceive this activity as part of their domain of responsibilities. Thus, community colleges offer the broadest array of ESL services because they perceive ESL as integral to their mission of serving community needs. Several of the community colleges visited had strong traditions of never turning anyone away and therefore were offering ESL well below the postsecondary level, in one case down to the third grade level and in other cases down to the eighth grade level. Respondents from four-year institutions varied in their willingness to turn away students with limited English skills. Even within institutions, we saw little consensus about the college's responsibility for upgrading students' language skills. Nonetheless, a slim majority of faculty and administrators within the baccalaureate institutions visited believed that the college's responsibilities extended only to giving students a chance to succeed, recognizing that some—and perhaps many—would fail. The outcome was that four-year institutions offered a limited array of ESL courses. In contrast, ESL instructors and student support staff in these institutions were more likely to argue for expanded ESL, providing a wider "safety net" for immigrant students.

OTHER CONSTRAINTS

Across all institutions studied, the continued growth of ESL was constrained, and in a few cases reversed, by a number of factors. These factors included gaps between faculty and staff perceptions of students' need and actual student demand for ESL and stalemates in decisionmaking due to conflicting views about the appropriate role and organization of ESL within undergraduate education.

Need Versus Demand for ESL

Despite the general perception that immigrant students' English was inadequate for college-level studies, negative attitudes at visited sites toward ESL courses among students and some counseling staff constrained growth of ESL. Across most of the campuses visited, immigrant students were described as eager to fulfill degree requirements, graduate, and join the work force. Thus, many immigrant students tried to minimize their participation in ESL, which slowed growth of ESL particularly in relation to the perceived need for ESL by faculty. Some immigrant students bypassed ESL assessment and placement procedures altogether, others appealed their ESL placements, and few completed more than the minimum amount of ESL course work required by their institutions. Arguments by faculty and staff that better English skills would improve students' learning and career opportunities were less than compelling for students struggling to balance the demands of school against family and work responsibilities. Academic counselors in two community colleges also discouraged the growth of ESL programs. These counselors encouraged students to try courses other than ESL, often against the advice of the ESL instructors. Counselors in these community colleges believed that the ESL department "held onto students too long" and hindered their degree progress.

Ambivalence and Conflicts Regarding Program Design

An important element of the institutional response to immigrants is widespread disagreement and institutional ambivalence about how to provide college-level ESL instruction. This lack of agreement is an obstacle to change since there is no predominant model or vision to guide decisionmaking.

Even among respondents within the same institution, we heard a profusion of conflicting perceptions and values related to ESL. For example, some ESL program leaders were disappointed that English faculty were reluctant to teach ESL and instead preferred "higher-level" courses; yet others complained that individuals without formal training in ESL were being asked to teach ESL classes. Some respondents noted that ESL programs were growing disproportionately to other academic and support services within the institution; others within the same school complained that ESL programs were held back from potential growth. Some believed that ESL should not suffer from the stigma of remediation; others believed that students needed to complete ESL courses before they could succeed in other courses. Even as academic counselors in some community colleges contended that ESL instructors held onto students too long, others within the same institution complained that students needed more ESL instruction before they could hope to complete college-level course work.

UNRESOLVED ISSUES

As immigrant enrollments lead to growth in the need for ESL programs, institutions are confronting a number of unresolved issues related to higher education responsibilities to immigrant students.

How much ESL instruction is enough? An influx of immigrants, many with limited English skills, raises questions about whether institutions should add new, lower-level ESL programs to serve these students, as opposed to referring them elsewhere or allowing them to try to succeed in college without a full range of ESL services. This question was particularly acute for community colleges that prided themselves on serving the entire community.

Is ESL course work remedial? To the extent that ESL instruction is viewed as remedial, it will provide few credits toward graduation and will not fulfill degree requirements. As such, students who enroll in ESL classes risk lengthening their time to degree and the overall costs of their college education. ESL instructors were reluctant to characterize ESL instruction as "remedial." They have support for this perspective from the U.S. Department of Education, which does not consider ESL instruction remedial for purposes of determining stu-

dents' financial aid eligibility. Most faculty and administrators, however, considered ESL programs to be a form of remediation.

Should ESL instruction be required? Advocates of required ESL
courses asserted that such policies conserve individual and institutional resources by avoiding placing students in courses where they
are likely to fail. On one hand, required ESL instruction may ensure
that college graduates achieve some minimal level of English ability,
thereby providing a form of quality assurance in undergraduate education. On the other hand, required ESL instruction increases time
to degree and costs of college. Additionally, many respondents were
reluctant to recommend more requirements, particularly in the absence of compelling evidence for the effectiveness of ESL instruction
on increasing retention and graduation rates.

Do ESL programs have the appropriate tools? Particularly when institutions require students to enroll in ESL classes, valid and reliable assessment instruments are essential. Yet the need for quality control
and equity in assessment often conflicts with the need for local control over curriculum, pedagogy, course structures, and assessment
systems. With each school offering different levels of ESL instruction, different credit policies, and different assessment systems, it is
not surprising that instructors in each location were overwhelmed
with the demands of developing their own curricula and assessment
tools. However, few had considered strategies that could reduce local burden without sacrificing local control. Information-sharing,
including central databanks of tests and materials, is just one strategy
that could help ESL departments and faculty avoid "reinventing the
wheel."

*How can articulation between ESL programs and other departments,
schools, and institutions be increased?* One of the weaknesses of
many ESL programs, particularly in schools that have ESL departments, is a lack of articulation between ESL and other aspects of the
institution or higher education system. Specific articulation issues
include the following:

- *Articulation among institutions.* Students who transfer between
  institutions may have difficulty gaining credit for prior ESL work
  and may also have difficulty determining the appropriate level of
  ESL instruction in which to enroll in their new institution. ESL

courses that provide elective credit toward graduation at one institution might be considered noncredit at another; ESL courses that fulfill prerequisites for freshman English at one college might not be accepted as a prerequisite at another institution. Courses with the same name or number may have very different content at different institutions.

- *Articulation between educational levels.* Respondents in four-year institutions observed that community college ESL courses did not adequately prepare transfer students for the demands of college. Respondents recommended that four-year institutions and their feeder institutions work together to improve ESL curricula and instruction for transfer students.

- *Articulation between adult schools and postsecondary institutions.* In theory, adult schools (typically run by local school districts) offer basic ESL instruction, and community colleges offer more advanced ESL courses. In practice, the distinction is less clear. The result is that, in some locations, we observed a gap in ESL services, so that those who needed more than basic English but less than college preparatory courses were underserved; in other locations, we observed redundancy between community colleges and adult schools. Both situations speak to the need for better coordination among ESL providers.

- *Articulation between credit and noncredit ESL programs.* Community colleges generally lack "cross walks" from noncredit to credit ESL programs. In one community college, for example, fewer than one percent of those taking ESL in the noncredit program subsequently enrolled in for-credit courses. Although the majority of those enrolling in ESL classes in community colleges may have neither the desire nor the preparation to obtain a college degree, the absence of articulation mechanisms inevitably means some loss of opportunity.

Chapter Six

COCURRICULAR PROGRAMS

The logic underlying the nonacademic component of American higher education reflects the long-standing tradition of developing well-rounded students. In addition, the role of cocurricular programs has evolved over time, moving away from the principle of in loco parentis toward a focus on morality and discipline and toward a broader, educational role (Garland, 1985). Today, cocurricular activities usually serve at least two purposes. First, such programs can support and extend the goals of the formal curriculum by helping students develop skills in leadership, cooperation, organization, and conflict resolution. Second, cocurricular programs and services improve retention and achievement by helping students overcome nonacademic obstacles to their success in college such as poor health, emotional stress, or career indecision.

The cocurricular component of undergraduate education can be divided into two categories: support services and extracurricular activities. Support services include career guidance, psychological counseling, health services, residential programs and services, and services for special populations such as women, ethnic minority students, students with disabilities, reentering students, or international students. These services are typically funded by the institutions, organized into departments or units, and staffed by professional service providers. Extracurricular programs are designed to enable students to affiliate with peers and pursue their interests outside the classroom. These typically include an array of student associations such as fraternities and sororities, academic clubs, ethnic or cultural associations, and special interest-based clubs, as well as intramural athletics, cultural programs, student government, and student media. Student associations are typically organized by students, with some institutional oversight.[1]

Even public institutions receive little guidance from legislatures or their governing boards regarding cocurricular programs; what programs they offer and how the programs are funded and structured are usually left to individual institutional preference. Community colleges, with a highly transient population of commuter students, may offer little more than short-term academic and career counseling services. Four-year colleges and universities with substantial numbers of undergraduates living on or near the campus stand at the other extreme. These schools may have hundreds of extracurricular programs and extensive student support services.

COCURRICULAR NEEDS OF IMMIGRANTS

Many observers expect immigrants to have special needs for cocurricular support. A primary concern is that lack of acculturation, and the acculturation process itself, can generate psychological stress that hinders adjustment to the college environment (Fernandez, 1988; Searles and Ward, 1990). Psychological counseling, then, is expected to help immigrants cope with acculturative stress. Counseling may also be especially needed by refugees, some of whom may experience posttraumatic stresses. For similar reasons, immigrants may face particular challenges related to career development. For example, immigrants may especially need coaching for job interviews, for which an understanding of Western values and interpersonal styles is particularly important. In this way, career counseling can become a vehicle for cultural assimilation. Student clubs and associations also may meet immigrants' needs. Peer support may be helpful in coping with acculturative stress and in bridging the contrasting cultures of home and school. Moreover, such activities offer opportunities to further the assimilation process by conveying

---

[1]Arrangements vary, however, and community colleges in particular may manage student clubs as well as support services. Funding for support services and extracurricular programs also varies across institutions. Sources of support may include special student fees as well as institutions' general funds derived from state appropriation, tuition, and education fees. Some services and programs also charge fees for service or membership, seek donations from individuals or corporations, or hold fundraising events.

skills in group participation and civic practices (e.g., student government).

INSTITUTIONAL RESPONSES TO IMMIGRATION

Across the institutions and systems visited in this study, we found only a handful of cocurricular services or activities that directly targeted immigrant students. The limited number of programs that did target this group were initiated by individual staff or faculty members, and their continued existence was, at best, tentative.

Language-Based Programs

Most commonly, schools attempted to serve immigrants by offering programs in languages of the dominant groups. Several schools we interviewed, for example, provided orientation sessions for students and parents in the language of the predominant immigrant group(s) for the region. Others hired bilingual and bicultural staff in service departments. However, some specialized services, (e.g., career and psychological counseling) reported difficulty finding qualified immigrant applicants.[2]

Support Services for Ethnic Groups

The colleges we visited expected immigrant students in need of support to use existing support services without special accommodations.[3] Although they did not target immigrants, all institutions we visited offered targeted support services for the traditionally disad-

---

[2]In addition to the staff of campus-based support services, respondents reported that ESL and other sympathetic faculty also offered substantial support and assistance to immigrant students. Since faculty often provided such support to nonimmigrant students, it is not clear that immigrants received more special attention than their native-born counterparts, but they were not overlooked.

[3]Some of the community colleges we visited offered noncredit amnesty programs and programs for recently arrived refugees and immigrants. Such special programs, however, did not address the needs or interests of students aspiring to the baccalaureate. For example, one community college offered their for-credit and amnesty/refugee programs on separate campuses, located several miles away from one another. Programs for immigrants were not included in this study unless they were relevant to students in for-credit programs.

vantaged ethnic groups in their student populations. In practice, immigrants were sometimes the primary beneficiaries of such services. For example, one university offered a support group for Asian students on academic probation; most of the group members were immigrants with significant English language difficulties. More often, however, immigrants were perceived to be less likely than native-born students to participate in these services. For example, Caribbean immigrants did not generally attend services and programs designed for black students.

Student Associations

All the institutions in our study sponsored some cultural and ethnic student associations. On each campus, the number of such associations ranged from under 10 to over 30. Although student associations are prohibited from restricting membership on the basis of race or ethnicity, in practice, membership in many groups is ethnically homogeneous. However, it is not homogeneous with regard to immigrant experience. Most members were unlikely to be immigrants, and we found few associations geared toward first-generation immigrants only.

Respondents reported that immigrants faced a number of barriers that are likely to limit their participation in extracurricular associations. The primary obstacle to participation was time since many immigrants had both work and family responsibilities. In addition, some immigrant cultures did not emphasize participation in extracurricular activities. Other immigrants were encouraged by their families to restrict contacts to those of their same culture or ethnicity, thereby reducing the scope of extracurricular opportunities available to them.

PERCEIVED NEED FOR TARGETED PROGRAMS

Almost all respondents from student affairs departments believed that immigrants could benefit from greater participation in cocurricular activities and services. For example, respondents noted that immigrants might experience more difficulty finding jobs if they remained uninvolved in extracurricular activities. Career advancement, as well, could be constrained for immigrants who did not take advantage of opportunities in college to develop their interpersonal and communication skills. Further, respondents with a counseling background were concerned that immigrants may have considerable unmet needs for psychological assistance.

While they believed that immigrants stood to gain a great deal from participation in cocurricular programs, respondents generally agreed that immigrants are reluctant participants. More specifically, respondents at 12 of the 14 institutions we visited believed that immigrant students were, relative to other students, less likely to use support services and less likely to join extracurricular activities. Those immigrant students who did become involved in campus activities, moreover, tended to select activities that limited their contact to other students of the same culture or ethnicity.

Empirical information about immigrants' participation in and attitudes toward campus life is lacking. Only two of 14 campuses visited for this study had systematically collected data about immigrant students' use of support services. In both cases, immigrants were roughly at parity with other students in their use of support services. Similarly, despite widespread assumptions that immigrants experience a "chilly" campus climate, none of the campuses we visited had systematically assessed immigrant students' attitudes toward the campus, although most had conducted recent campus climate studies.

PERCEIVED APPROPRIATENESS OF DEVELOPING TARGETED PROGRAMS

Despite widespread acknowledgment of immigrant student needs, campuses were reluctant to tailor cocurricular services and activities specifically to immigrant students. Most respondents believed that immigrant needs did not differ markedly from those of other groups, and thus they saw little need for new or different cocurricular offerings. Perhaps most important, campuses were growing increasingly sensitive to the issue of "balkanization" and were reluctant to create programs that would further divide their students.

Problems Are Common to Many Groups

While they acknowledged the needs of immigrants, respondents did not believe that providing programs specifically targeted to immigrants was equitable or necessary. Rather, they believed that with few exceptions, immigrant needs were shared by many student groups, including low-income students who must balance work with school and minority students who may feel alienated or excluded from traditional campus services and activities. Because ethnicity and income are the predominant identifiers for these groups, they saw no reason why immigrants should not be adequately served by the existing programs designed for the whole student population or for ethnic or economic subgroups.

Growing Concerns Regarding Campus Fragmentation

Any attempt to develop specialized programs that targeted immigrant students must address the question of campus fragmentation or "balkanization." One or more respondents within 11 of the 14 campuses reported growing concern that, in conflict with the institutional goal of developing understanding and patterns of cooperation across groups, students were choosing to limit their informal associations to peers of the same ethnic, racial, or experiential background. Respondents feared that if they provided special services to immigrants, they would at the same time further fragment campus groupings by creating yet another special group that might discourage student cooperation across groups. Many long-term student affairs administrators were concluding that some institutional policies and practices, for example, support services for designated ethnic groups or financial support for group publications or events, were instrumental in encouraging the growing fragmentation, and they were therefore particularly reluctant to consider support for new groups.

OTHER CONSTRAINTS

Campuses have a number of additional reasons for not targeting immigrants in their provision of cocurricular services, including pervasive confusion regarding distinctions between immigrant and foreign students, the low demand for such services, and resource constraints.

Foreign Versus Immigrant Students

Widespread confusion about the distinction between immigrant and international students constrained campus responses to immigrants. Most of the institutions visited had student affairs offices for international students. Some respondents assumed that such offices served immigrant students. They did not understand that these offices generally restricted services only to students with F-1 or J-1 visas, who pay high out-of-state tuition that may subsidize other institutional activities.

Demand for Cocurricular Services and Activities

The majority of student affairs respondents noted that immigrant students themselves rarely express strong interest in expanding services. Several of these respondents explained that institutions respond to "squeaky wheels," implementing new programs and services in response to student demand. A lack of advocacy by immigrant students for special services, then, encouraged student life administrators to overlook their needs in planning and programming.

Similarly, immigrants were perceived as largely removed from intergroup conflicts and therefore did not demand attention from administrators. Although interview respondents described situations in which immigrant students were taunted or harassed, these were for the most part seen as isolated incidents and not part of a larger pattern of intergroup conflict or systematic discrimination. Similarly, while respondents also described situations in which immigrant students expressed biased attitudes toward other groups, these too were seen as isolated events and not a pattern that demanded administrative intervention. In contrast, administrators were typically quick to act in response to conflicts involving native-born Hispanic, African American, or white students because of a concern that misunderstandings or disagreements among individuals could quickly escalate.

Institutions were also hampered in their responses to immigrant students by their limited control over the activities of many student groups (including funding to student groups provided by student government) and by the pervasiveness of ethnic and cultural programming, often institutionalized in such components of campus life as orientation, graduation, counseling, residential life, and media.

Resource Constraints

In addition, most of the campuses we visited simply did not have the resources to increase immigrant participation in cocurricular activities. Many respondents recommended that campuses should hire staff and faculty representative of the diversity in the student body. These respondents contended that immigrant students would be more likely to use counseling or other support services if they could work with staff from their own background.[4] However, severe fiscal constraints facing many of the institutions visited, coupled with difficulty recruiting immigrants into student life positions, made this recommendation difficult to implement. In fact, many staff in these positions were being laid off. For example, one institution we visited had been forced to lay off about one-quarter of its counseling staff. Since layoffs were based on seniority (with the least senior laid off first), several Asian counselors were dismissed. Another institution had hoped to recruit an Asian career counselor but could find no Asian applicants for the position.

GUIDING VALUES

Whose values should be applied when counseling immigrant students—the values of the student or those generally accepted by the student affairs community? Many of the values underlying the activities of student affairs staff and administrators may not be shared by immigrants or their families. For example, most student affairs professionals value individual autonomy and strive to help students achieve independence from their families. Students are encouraged to interact with a wide range of peers (both male and female), to

---

[4]The few immigrant student affairs staff with whom we met were in fact inundated with requests for assistance from immigrant students.

practice assertive forms of communication, and to explore a range of possible majors and careers before selecting the path that "feels" best for them. All of these values may directly contradict those of other cultures; yet they are the values of the new, receiving country and they will be the values of the workplace in which the graduating student finds him or herself. How should schools balance respect for the immigrant student's values and recognition of the stress that change will cause with encouraging, even pressing students into cultural assimilation?

Another question concerns how student affairs divisions should balance the dual values of ethnic and racial group solidarity and support with intergroup cooperation. The prevailing view was that students should ideally belong to both homogeneous and heterogeneous groups, but most respondents agreed that this was not occurring. They did not agree, however, on the causes of the observed fragmentation of the campus community, nor did they agree on the institution's responsibility and role for promoting different patterns of intergroup association. Questions that were raised by these issues but that remain unanswered include the following: Does institutional support of group identity exacerbate a problem? Does such support on the basis of ethnic grouping contribute to the retention and future success of disadvantaged students? Does fragmentation significantly limit the development of respect and cooperative habits among students of different backgrounds?

Uncertainty about how vigorously institutions should promote their values over the values of other groups or those of individuals limited the degree to which student affairs professionals intervened to promote immigrant participation in campus life.

Chapter Seven

FINDINGS AND DISCUSSION

In describing how colleges and universities were responding to the rise in U.S. immigration and what perceptions drove their responses, we find that the large and diverse immigrant population highlights several pivotal, unresolved tensions facing the higher education sector.

FINDINGS

Synthesizing findings from the respondents to our study, we discover diverse, important policy issues.

Immigrants were not a targeted population within any of the 14 campuses included in this study. Although ethnicity was a highly salient characteristic for all campus members, few thought of *immigrant* students as a group. In their numerous data collection efforts, most campuses collected few data on immigrant status. Similarly, in their direct dealings with students, faculty and staff reported rarely being aware of immigrant status. Few saw the failure to distinguish this population as a shortcoming.

To the degree that they voiced any opinion, respondents believed that immigrant students do better than native-born students. When pressed, respondents typically described immigrants as doing better academically than other students, and although they acknowledged some possible specific barriers to academic success, they suggested immigrants enjoyed more-than-compensating supports.

There was consistent opposition to the introduction of special support programs that target immigrant students. Respondents argued that the problems immigrants face are no different from those faced by many other students, and that other groups tend to be more disadvantaged than immigrants are. Many feared that targeting groups for special support would exacerbate campus fragmentation. Respondents also reported that immigrant students are reluctant to use existing programs and therefore did not expect them to use new services that might be developed for them.

Inadequate language skills were reported as the most outstanding problem shared by immigrants. Respondents generally agreed that inadequate language skills constituted the greatest barrier immigrants face in acquiring a sound postsecondary education. However, the agreement ended there. There was substantial disagreement about how faculty should respond to this problem and what responsibilities colleges and universities have for remediation.

In some settings, eligibility requirements for admissions and financial aid were poorly understood and unevenly implemented. Eligibility requirements for admission and for some forms of financial aid are a complex combination of statute, court rulings, and institutional policy. Moreover, requirements established by external bodies often conflict with institutional and staff values. The result has been uneven awareness and implementation.

The continuing increase in immigration strains some operations and functions, creating problems of efficiency and cost-effectiveness. This is most clearly seen within the admissions function of foreign transcript reviews but also applies to other areas, including financial aid and ESL.

The continuing increase in immigration adds to campus diversity. This diversity offers important educational opportunities but also raises new questions about the definitions and criteria for such commonly used designations as "underrepresented" or "disadvantaged."

The continuing increase in immigration highlights the salience of unresolved issues related to institutional responsibilities to students. These issues concern the importance of English language competency, the role of assessment, the significance of student participation in the campus community, and access for undocumented students or others who are not permanent residents.

UNRESOLVED CHALLENGES FACING INSTITUTIONS

While our case studies illuminate a number of important areas of agreement on the nations' campuses, they also highlight critical areas of strain or tension. Although these strains have not yet reached anything close to crisis proportions, they contribute to the pressures facing the higher education sector and demonstrate the difficulties the sector experiences in adapting to a changing environment. Further, left unaddressed, these problems are likely to increase and culminate in intervention by outside policymakers (e.g., state legislators).

To date, the challenges posed by immigration have not achieved a level of intensity that requires concerted intervention or response. Nonetheless, staff and faculty throughout the institution must cope with these challenges on a daily basis. Moreover, as immigrant enrollments increase, or as institutions experience new demands in other domains, these fairly low-level strains may grow in significance.

Efficiency in Operations

Effects of Immigration on Institutions. The continuing increase in immigration places greater burdens on staff in admissions offices because procedures for reviewing foreign transcripts are time-consuming and labor-intensive. Students are often disappointed in the outcomes of this process, which leads to appeals that require additional time and attention. As the number of immigrant applicants for admission increases, more staff may also be needed to verify or clarify student residence for fee purposes. The complexity of state policies render this task especially labor-intensive. The financial aid process is also more complex for immigrant students because of the need to verify visa status with the INS. As a result, financial aid offices need to spend more time processing applications from immigrant students. Increased immigration also leads to new burdens on ESL faculty through an increased need for, and complexity of, placement and diagnostic procedures and tools. ESL faculty spend substantial amounts of time trying to develop (or modify) instruments to articulate with the structure and goals of their curricula and the needs of their institution's student population.

Institutional Responses. Despite increasingly unwieldy processes and unsatisfying outcomes for both students and institutions, the schools we studied largely persisted in using established procedures and often resisted considering alternatives. To date, however, little thought has been devoted to developing alternatives that can fulfill institutional needs in a more efficient—and higher quality—manner.

Discussion. In the face of clear, and growing, inefficiencies in some operations, institutions continue to use more of the same procedures rather than modify their efforts or seek innovative solutions. Little thought has been devoted to new approaches that would improve both quality and efficiency. For example, interinstitutional cooperative alliances and the development of information clearinghouses appear promising but are receiving scant attention.

In the past, institutions were able to respond to increased workloads with more staff. Today, however, most public institutions operate in a climate of significant financial constraint. The challenge to institutions, then, lies in increasing efficiency and productivity because it is unlikely that growth in resources will keep up with growth in workload.

Increased Diversity

Effects of Immigration on Institutions. Rising immigration adds to campus diversity, increasing the ethnic, cultural, linguistic, and socioeconomic diversity that already characterizes American higher education. In so doing, immigration offers colleges and universities a rich educational resource, bringing students the opportunity to build their understanding of, appreciation for, and ability to work with people of different backgrounds and cultures from their own.

At the same time, however, immigration leads administrators, faculty, students, and community members to raise questions about how institutions should formulate goals and monitor the participation of students across ethnic and racial groups. The substantial differences in college enrollment between immigrants and native-born individuals of the same race or ethnicity challenge the assumptions behind the designation of certain groups as "disadvantaged" or "underrepresented." The logic of classifying all black or all Hispanic students as disadvantaged begins to break down, for example, when these ethnic groups include both immigrants with strong educational backgrounds and native-born students with relatively weak educational backgrounds. Similarly, the widespread exclusion of Asians from programs geared toward underrepresented ethnic groups can be challenged since specific Asian immigrant subgroups show low rates of college enrollment.

Institutional Responses. Despite growing within-group diversity linked to immigration, institutions continued to stress race and ethnicity for identifying "disadvantaged" or "underrepresented" students. Programs, services, and benefits that used race or ethnicity as a criterion for participation were perceived as leading to intergroup tensions. However, programs that used income or other criteria that were not related to race or ethnicity to determine eligibility were also criticized. Thus, politically acceptable alternatives to racial and ethnic considerations had not yet been discovered on the campuses we visited.

These institutions were, however, grappling with the choice of whether to consider cultural or ethnic subgroups in policymaking and thereby expand the categories used to track applications, admissions, enrollment, and retention. One California university, for example, had over a dozen categories for tracking Asian students and six for tracking Hispanic students. Roughly half the institutions studied had increased the number of racial or ethnic categories used for student tracking within the last five years.

Discussion. Within-group variation created by immigration renders illogical the practice of classifying all members of a particular racial or ethnic group as "disadvantaged" or "underrepresented" (or vice versa). The category "black," for example, on many campuses now includes the traditionally underrepresented group of African Americans, a group of Haitian immigrants who vary widely in their preparation for college, and a group of immigrants from other Caribbean or African nations who are often highly prepared for college. Should all of these students be eligible for the same services and programs? A similar question can be asked about the exclusion of Asians or white Eastern Europeans from some special programs and services.

Institutional responses to this diversity must stem from institutional goals and values. The exclusion of Cambodian immigrants from affirmative action programs, for example, is illogical if the goal of these programs is to contribute toward building the strongest possible workforce for the nation. The exclusion of certain immigrants would be more defensible, however, if the goal of such programs is to redress historical patterns of inequity and discrimination that blocked upward mobility and contributed to low rates of college enrollment among some groups over multiple generations. Further, an influx of immigrant students, many of whom are classified as economically or educationally disadvantaged or as members of underrepresented groups, raises questions about displacement. Displacement may occur either within or between ethnic groups. An example of the former is the possibility—one that none of the campuses we visited had empirically investigated—that programs designed to recruit and enroll African American students are increasingly serving Caribbean immigrants rather than native-born students. An example of the latter is the possibility—one that is supported by anecdotal evidence in the absence of empirical investigation—that, on some campuses, special admissions programs intended to provide access for a small number of promising students whose grades or test scores fall below official criteria are increasingly serving Asian immigrants with low verbal but high quantitative scores rather than the intended native-born students. The significance of displacement also depends upon the goals of the programs and services involved.

The trend toward increasing the number of ethnic categories used for student tracking is a potentially useful response to these concerns. On one hand, this approach reduces ambiguity in the data, allows institutions to select subgroups for special programs or focused outreach, and enables empirical investigation of displacement. On the other hand, this approach is awkward at best. There are scores of cultures and ethnicities represented on U.S. college campuses. At some point, the ability of a college to make sense of multiple categories of data and respond appropriately to the needs of each group breaks down.

Questions About Institutional Responsibilities

Effects of Immigration on Institutions. Increased immigration raises the salience of unresolved issues regarding institutional responsibilities to students both within and outside the classroom. These questions exist independent of the participation of immigrants; yet immigrant enrollments highlight and amplify them.

Increased immigration heightens awareness about whether English language mastery is important within undergraduate education. Although most case study respondents agreed that a baccalaureate degree from a U.S. institution should indicate that the recipient has strong verbal and written English skills, relatively few faculty were able or willing to adjust their teaching styles to assist students with limited proficiency in English. In addition, many faculty were reluctant to penalize immigrants who, despite communications difficulties, were able to complete the college curriculum. Thus, immigrant student participation reflects and arguably increases incongruence between institutional values (i.e., the importance of English language skills) and behavior (e.g., faculty grading practices).

Similarly, the increased immigration reflects and amplifies preexisting tensions related to student assessment. Institutions that require students to pass reading or writing competency tests as a requirement for graduation were particularly marked by debate on this issue, with some faculty and administrators defending the tests as essential to maintaining standards and others arguing that the tests disproportionately and unfairly penalized immigrants.

The growth in need and demand for ESL instruction linked to immigration has created concerns among administrators about how to balance ESL programs against other programs and services and where to draw the boundaries of institutional responsibility for providing ESL instruction. Unresolved issues include the extent of ESL instruction needed for higher education ESL programs, whether ESL instruction should be mandated or optional, and how ESL courses should articulate with degree requirements.

Outside the classroom, immigrant enrollment in higher education was associated with increased numbers of student-organized cultural clubs, sometimes leading to increased competition for resources among all student groups. Further, the cultural diversity that accompanies immigrant participation raises the likelihood that students' values, rooted in their own cultural traditions and beliefs, conflict with institutional values, rooted largely in Western cultural traditions.

Finally, campuses located in regions with large numbers of undocumented immigrants, or immigrants who have applied for asylum but have not yet had a hearing, faced questions about their responsibilities to students without permanent residence status. These institutions must decide how to implement state and federal policies regarding fees and financial aid, how to respond to policymakers on issues related to nonpermanent resident students, and whether to attempt to compensate for public policies through use of institutional scholarships.

Institutional Responses. Fully 13 of the 14 institutions studied had made no systematic effort to determine or clarify institutional responsibilities for ensuring immigrant student access and academic success. With regard to English language skills, institutions offered only limited guidance to faculty about how to respond to immigrants and even less tangible support. Discrepancies between institutional values and practices were infrequently noted and even less frequently addressed.

None of the campuses we visited had systematically considered the implications of immigrant enrollment for cocurricular services and programs. Thus, in seeking to promote students' personal growth and development, student affairs staff risked inadvertently exacerbating acculturative stress for some immigrant students.

Finally, implementation of state and, to a lesser extent, federal policies related to immigrant students who lack permanent residence status was erratic and unsystematic. One reason for this inconstancy was that many staff, faculty, administrators, and students were confused about the intent and meaning of the policies as well as institutional procedures for implementing them. A second reason for erratic implementation was the diversity of attitudes toward these policies. Staff and faculty who assumed advocacy roles on behalf of nonpermanent residents applied different interpretations to policies and employed less rigorous validation methods than others did. A clear and consistent understanding of the manner in which the institution was to balance the goal of access for disadvantaged students with the goal of complying with public policy was lacking in 12 of the 14 institutions we studied.

Discussion. These findings indicate that institutions have not clarified their core values and, as a result, cannot determine their responsibilities toward immigrant—or other—students. This ambiguity and uncertainty has at least four negative effects. First, erratic implementation of institutional policies or values raises questions of equity. Educational inequities occur when one professor penalizes immigrant students for difficulties in written and spoken English while another ignores these issues. Current practices related to nonpermanent residents also risk inadvertently perpetuating educational inequities at the individual level, since one student may gain access while another, in the same situation, may be denied access.

Second, institutions send double messages to immigrant students and the broader community, possibly increasing student stress and certainly leading to confusion about institutional values. For example, although good writing skills were emphasized in virtually every school we visited, few faculty were prepared to provide immigrant students with assistance in improving their writing skills and most were reluctant or lacked any means to force immigrants (or others) into ESL or remedial classes. Under such conditions, the institution sends a mixed message about the importance of writing skills. Similarly, student affairs professionals inadvertently send mixed messages about multicultural appreciation, on the one hand encouraging students to deepen their understanding and acceptance of diverse cultures yet on the other hand embracing a set of values that are rooted in Western cultural traditions.

Third, the lack of clear values risks reductions in program quality. At worst, for example, the value of the baccalaureate is degraded when students with weak English skills receive a diploma and enter the job market unprepared to meet the requirements or expectations of employers. Ambiguity about the importance of English language proficiency or about the standards students are expected to achieve poses obvious problems for the design of ESL programs. Further, cocurricular programs and services are weakened by inconsistent or unclear goals or values.

Fourth, a lack of clear values increases the difficulties institutions face in making trade-offs among alternative policy and programmatic directions. For example, the level of resources that should be devoted to ESL as opposed to other activities is ultimately a question of values. Is it more important for a four-year institution to support ESL for limited-English-proficiency students or tutoring for educationally underprepared students? Should limited classroom space be devoted to ESL or to other educational activities? Furthermore, ambiguity about institutional responsibilities to students without permanent residence status prevents institutions from considering the trade-offs involved in various policy alternatives. For example, should institutional financial aid be used to support students who are not eligible for state or federal financial aid, or should it be used for merit scholarships for highly achieving students regardless of their eligibility for other forms of aid? Institutional policies and practices related to immigrants inevitably also involve trade-offs among services to individual students since resources are limited. Rather than make these trade-offs based on a thoughtful analysis of the institutional role and capacity, many institutions are instead avoiding this work and, by default, allowing individual staff or faculty to determine appropriate action. Confusion about institutional values within many institutions enables staff to administer their responsibilities in the manner congruent with their personal values.

Several factors account for the general lack of clarity. Some institutions that have only recently experienced an influx of immigrants have not faced the need to address these issues until quite recently; others have only recently experienced significant changes in immigrant characteristics (e.g., family income or English language skills). Higher education leaders are facing considerable demands from the public, and, so long as immigrant students are not overtly problematic, other issues are assigned a higher priority for institutional attention.

In addition, discussions about values are often contentious, and institutional leaders avoid addressing these issues because of concerns that they will engender conflict. Similarly, given growing anti-immigrant sentiments, campus efforts to address immigrant student issues are likely to lead to policies or procedures that are more restrictive than current practices—an outcome that is anathema to many faculty, staff, and administrators who strive to increase access and academic success for *all* students, especially disadvantaged students. The rancorous discussions that could ensue might also capture the attention of policymakers and bring negative publicity to institutions. Thus, some institutional leaders have avoided embarking on a process to clarify institutional responsibilities because they believe that the process could be harmful to both students and institutions.

Ultimately, however, the confusion manifested on campuses reflects the confusion in the society at large. The values guiding national immigration policy are unclear, and the American people are increasingly divided about immigration issues. To expect colleges and universities to resolve these issues in the absence of clear policy directions at a national level is to assign these institutions a substantial, and possibly misdirected, challenge.

FUTURE DIRECTIONS

In the absence of clear problems on campuses and without strong political pressures regarding immigrant students, administrators have turned to other, more pressing, issues and concerns. Most of our respondents would probably have agreed with one student affairs administrator who responded to a question about the need for more attention to immigrant students by saying, "The problem is that we might be raising a consciousness that doesn't need to be raised."

The widespread assumptions and beliefs about immigrant students, however, are unconfirmed by empirical data. Unchecked, these assumptions may result in unfair practices and reduced educational quality. Few institutions regularly studied trends in immigrant student enrollment, retention, and graduation rates. None had examined trends in TOEFL scores for immigrant students. None had compared outcomes for immigrants based on length of residence in the United States or based on country of origin. None had examined the effectiveness of ESL instruction in promoting higher achievement and graduation rates. None had explored whether immigrants were displacing native-born students. And none had asked immigrant students about their needs and perceptions of the campus environment.

The dramatic growth in immigration to the United States and the critical role of higher education in promoting economic assimilation suggest that institutional leaders should focus greater attention on issues related to immigrant students. Needed information includes descriptive statistics about immigrants' enrollment and retention in college, attitudinal and needs assessment studies, and evaluations of student outcomes and the effectiveness of remedial and ESL programs. In this way, institutions can determine if administrator and faculty perceptions and beliefs about immigrants provide an accurate foundation for future policy and program development.

BIBLIOGRAPHY

American Association of State Colleges and Universities and National Association of State Universities and Land-Grant Colleges, *A Challenge of Change: Public, Four-Year Higher Education Enrollment Lessons from the 1980s for the 1990s*, Washington, D.C., 1992.

Asian Pacific American Education Advisory Committee, *Enriching California's Future: Asian Pacific Americans in the CSU*, Long Beach, Calif.: Office of the Chancellor, California State University, November 1990.

The Aspen Institute, "Closing the Disconnect in American Higher Education: A Summary of a Seminar's Discussion," The Aspen Institute, ed., *American Higher Education: Purposes, Problems and Public Perceptions*, Queenstown, Md.: The Aspen Institute, 1992, pp. 1–16.

Astin, Alexander W., *What Matters in College? Four Critical Years Revisited*, San Francisco, Calif.: Jossey-Bass, 1993.

Bach, Robert L., *Changing Relations: Newcomers and Established Residents in U.S. Communities*, New York: Ford Foundation, 1993.

Benjamin, R. W., S. J. Carroll, M. Jacobi, C. S. Krop, and M. Shires, *The Redesign of Governance in Higher Education*, Santa Monica, Calif.: RAND, MR-222-LE, 1993.

Bers, Trudy, "English Proficiency, Course Patterns, and Academic Achievements of Limited-English-Proficient Community College Students," *Research in Higher Education*, Vol. 35, pp. 209–235, 1994.

Bloom, Allan, *The Closing of the American Mind*, New York, N.Y.: Simon & Schuster, 1987.

Borjas, George J., *Friends or Strangers: The Impact of Immigrants on the U.S. Economy*, New York, N.Y.: Basic Books, 1990.

Breneman, David W., "Sweeping Painful Changes," *The Chronicle of Higher Education*, Vol. 42, pp. B1–B2, September 8, 1995.

Bureau of the Census, *We the American . . . Foreign Born*, Washington, D.C.: U.S. Department of Commerce, Economics and Statistics Administration, 1993.

Butler, Johnnella, and Betty Schmitz, "Ethnic Studies, Women's Studies, and Multiculturalism," *Change*, Vol. 24, 1992, pp. 36–41.

Byron, William J., "Needed: Creative Policy Ideas to Resolve the Competing Claims of Quality, Diversity, and Efficiency in Higher Education," David H. Finifter, Roger G. Baldwin, and John R. Thelin, eds., *The Uneasy Public Policy Triangle in Higher Education: Quality, Diversity, and Budgetary Efficiency*, New York, N.Y.: American Council on Education and Macmillan Publishing Company, 1991, pp. 177–188.

Carnegie Foundation for the Advancement of Teaching, *Campus Life: In Search of Community*, Lawrenceville, N.J.: Princeton University Press, 1990.

Carter, Deborah J., and Reginald Wilson, *Minorities in Higher Education 1994: Thirteenth Annual Status Report*, Washington, D.C.: American Council on Education, 1995.

Chen, Xuya, and Wu Hong, "Studying in the United States: The Experience of Chinese Students at Queens College," *Asian/American Center Working Papers*, Queens College, City University of New York, 1989.

The Chronicle of Higher Education, Almanac Issue, September 1, 1994.

The Chronicle of Higher Education, Almanac Issue, September 1, 1995.

Clotfelter, Charles T., et al., *Economic Challenges in Higher Education*, Chicago, Ill.:   University of Chicago Press for the National Bureau of Economic Research, 1991.

Cohen, A. M., and F. B. Brawer, *The American Community College*, San Francisco, Calif.: Jossey-Bass, 1989.

Davis, Camas, "Student Cuts: Contract with America," E-mail correspondence of February 23, 1995.

Dunlap, Jonathan C., *America's Newcomers: A State and Local Policymakers' Guide to Immigration and Immigrant Policy*, Washington, D.C.:   National Conference of State Legislatures, 1993.

Dunlap, Jonathan C., and Ann Morse, "States Sue Feds to Recover Immigration Costs," *National Conference of State Legislatures Legisbrief*, Vol. 3, 1995.

Duran, Bernadine J., and Rafaela E. Weffer, "Immigrants' Aspirations, High School Process, and Academic Outcomes," *American Educational Research Journal*, Vol. 29, No. 1, 1992, pp. 163–181.

Eaton, Judith S., "The Evolution of Access Policy: 1965–1990," The Aspen Institute, ed., *American Higher Education: Purposes, Problems and Public Perceptions*, Queenstown, Md.: The Aspen Institute, Program in Education for a Changing Society, 1992, pp. 141–158.

Fernandez, Mary S., "Issues in Counseling Southeast-Asian Students," *Journal of Multicultural Counseling and Development*, Vol. 16, 1988, pp. 157–166.

"Financing American Higher Education: Overview and Pressures," a background paper prepared for the Business–Higher Education Forum, February 1994.

Finifter, David H., Roger G. Baldwin, and John R. Thelin, *The Uneasy Public Policy Triangle in Higher Education: Quality, Diversity, and Budgetary Efficiency*, New York, N.Y.: American Council on Education and Macmillan Publishing Company, 1991.

Finn, Chester E., "Why are People Beating Up on Higher Education?" The Aspen Institute, ed., *American Higher Education: Purposes, Problems and Public Perceptions*, Queenstown, Md.: The Aspen Institute, Program in Education for a Changing Society, 1992, pp. 17–42.

Fullerton, Howard N., Jr., "New Labor Force Projections, Spanning 1988 to 2000," *Monthly Labor Review*, Vol. 112, No. 11, November 1989, pp. 3–12.

Furnham, Adrian, and Naznin Alibhai, "Value Differences in Foreign Students," *International Journal of Intercultural Relations*, Vol. 9, 1986, pp. 365–375.

Gappa, Judith M., "Part-Time Faculty: Higher Education at a Crossroads," *ASHE-ERIC Higher Education Research Report No. 3*, Washington, D.C.: Association for the Study of Higher Education, ED 251 058, 1984.

Garland, Peter H., "Serving More Than Students: A Critical Need for College Student Personnel Services," *ASHE-ERIC Higher Education Report No. 7*, Washington, D.C.: Association for the Study of Higher Education, 1985.

Garland, Peter H., and Thomas W. Grace, "New Perspectives for Student Affairs Professionals: Evolving Realities, Responsibilities, and Roles," *ASHE-ERIC Higher Education Report No. 7*, Washington, D.C.: Association for the Study of Higher Education, 1993.

Graham, Morris A., "Acculturative Stress Among Polynesian, Asian and American Students on the Brigham Young University—Hawaii Campus," *International Journal of Multicultural Relations*, Vol. 7, 1983, pp. 79–103.

Green, Madeleine F., ed., *Minorities on Campus: A Handbook for Enhancing Diversity*, Washington, D.C.: American Council on Education, 1989.

Grubb, W. Norton, Torry Dickinson, Lirraine Giordana, and Kail Kaplan, *Betwixt and Between: Education, Skills, and Employment in Sub-Baccalaureate Labor Markets*, Berkeley, Calif.: National

Center for Research in Vocational Education, University of California, Berkeley, MDS-470, December 1992.

Gutmann, Amy, "What Counts as Quality in Higher Education?" David H. Finifter, Roger G. Baldwin, and John R. Thelin, eds., *The Uneasy Public Policy Triangle in Higher Education: Quality, Diversity, and Budgetary Efficiency*, New York, N.Y.: American Council on Education and Macmillan Publishing Company, 1991, pp. 45–53.

Handel, Stephen J., and Dario J. Caloss, *A Declaration of Community: Report of the Universitywide Campus Community Task Force*, Oakland, Calif.: University of California, July 1993.

Hart, P. J., and M. Jacobi, *From Gatekeeper to Advocate: Transforming the Role of the School Counselor*, New York, N.Y.: The College Board, 1992.

Harvey, Lee, and Diana Green, "Defining Quality," *Assessment and Evaluation in Higher Education*, Vol. 18, No. 1, 1993, pp. 9–34.

Hauptman, Arthur M., "Quality and Access in Higher Education: The Impossible Dream?" The Aspen Institute, ed., *American Higher Education: Purposes, Problems and Public Perceptions*, Queenstown, Md.: The Aspen Institute, Program in Education for a Changing Society, 1992, pp. 115–140.

Hauptman, Arthur M., and Maureen A. McLaughlin, "Is the Goal of College Access Being Met?" The Aspen Institute, ed., *American Higher Education: Purposes, Problems and Public Perceptions*, Queenstown, Md.: The Aspen Institute, Program in Education for a Changing Society, 1992, pp. 159–186.

Healy, Patrick, "Budget Cuts Threaten Programs in English as a Second Language," *The Chronicle of Higher Education*, June 16, 1995, p. A26.

Hearn, James C., and Carolyn P. Griswold, "State-Level Centralization and Policy Innovation in U.S. Postsecondary Education," *Educational Evaluation and Policy Analysis*, Vol. 16, No. 2, 1994, pp. 161–190.

Higher Education Publications, *The HEP . . . Higher Education Directory*, Washington, D.C., 1995.

Ignash, Jan M., "ESL Population and Program Patterns in Community Colleges," *ERIC Digest*, EDO-JC-92-05, December 1992.

Immigrant Policy Project, "Seven State Fiscal Study: Impacts of Undocumented Immigrants," *Immigrant Policy News*, Vol. 1, No. 2, November 9, 1994, p. 2.

Institute for the Study of Social Change, *The Diversity Project: Final Report*, Berkeley, Calif.: University of California, Berkeley, 1991.

Jacobi, Maryann, *Student Services Assessment: Report on Undergraduate Student Problems*, Los Angeles, Calif.: Student Affairs Information and Research Office, University of California, Los Angeles, Fall 1989.

Kerschner, Lee R., "Immigration: Recognizing the Benefit, Meeting the Challenges," American Association of State Colleges and Universities, ed., *A Challenge of Change: Public Four-Year Higher Education Enrollment Lessons from the 1980s for the 1990s*, Washington, D.C.: American Association of State Colleges and Universities, 1992.

Kinnick, Mary K., and Mary F. Ricks, "Student Retention: Moving from Numbers to Action," *Research in Higher Education*, Vol. 34, No. 1, 1993, pp. 55–70.

Koretz, Daniel M., *Trends in the Postsecondary Enrollment of Minorities*, Santa Monica, Calif.: RAND, R-3948-FF, 1990.

Levine, Arthur, and Jeanette Cureton, "The Quiet Revolution: Eleven Facts About Multiculturalism and the Curriculum," *Change*, Vol. 24, 1992, pp. 24–29.

Lively, Kit, "Confronting 'Prop. 187': Measure Barring Services to Illegal Immigrants Poses Dilemma for California Colleges," *The Chronicle of Higher Education*, February 24, 1995, pp. A29–A30.

Mansfield, Wendy, Elizabeth Farris, and MacKnight Black, *College-Level Remedial Education in the Fall of 1989: Contractor Report*,

Washington D.C.:   U.S. Department of Education, Office of Education Research and Improvement, NCES 91-191, May 1991.

McDonnell, Lorraine M., and Paul T. Hill, *Newcomers in American Schools: Meeting the Educational Needs of Immigrant Youth*, Santa Monica, Calif.: RAND, MR-103-AWM/PRIP, 1993.

Mena, Francisco J., Amado M. Padilla, and Margarita Maldonado, "Acculturative Stress and Specific Coping Strategies Among Immigrant and Later Generation College Students," *Hispanic Journal of Behavioral Sciences*, Vol. 9, No. 2, 1987, pp. 207–225.

Merl, Jean, "Community College Fee Hike Hits Illegal Immigrants," *Los Angeles Times*, May 14, 1992, p. 3.

National Center for Education Statistics (NCES), *College-Level Remedial Education in the Fall of 1989: Contractor Report*, U.S. Department of Education, Office of Education Research and Improvement, NCES 91-191, 1991.

National Research Council (Ronald S. Fesco and Benjamin F. King), *Quality in Student Financial Aid Programs: A New Approach*, Washington, D.C.: National Academy Press, 1993.

Nettles, Michael T., "The Emerging National Policy Agenda on Higher Education Assessment: A Wake-Up Call," *The Review of Higher Education*, Vol. 18, No. 3, 1995, pp. 293–313.

Olivas, Michael A., "The Political Economy of Immigration, Intellectual Property, and Racial Harassment: Case Studies of the Implementation of Legal Change on Campus," *Journal of Higher Education*, Vol. 63, No. 5, 1992, pp. 570–598.

Padilla, Amado M., Monica Alvarez, and Kathryn J. Lindholm, "Generational Status and Personality Factors and Predictors of Stress in Students," *Hispanic Journal of Behavioral Sciences*, Vol. 8, No. 3, 1986, pp. 275–288.

Pascarella, Ernest T., and Patrick T. Terenzini, *How College Affects Students: Findings and Insights from Twenty Years of Research*, San Francisco, Calif.: Jossey-Bass, 1991.

Passel, Jeffrey S., Frank D. Bean, and Barry Edmonston, "Undocumented Migration Since IRCA: An Overall Assessment," Frank D. Bean, Barry Edmonston, and Jeffrey S. Passel, eds., *Undocumented Migration in the United States: IRCA and the Experience of the 1980s*, Washington, D.C.: The Urban Institute Press, pp. 251–266.

Pearson, Carol S., Donna L. Shavlik, and Judith G. Touchton, *Educating the Majority: Women Challenge Tradition in Higher Education*, New York, N.Y.: American Council on Education and Macmillan, 1989.

Pike, Gary R., "Lies, Damn Lies, and Statistics Revisited: A Comparison of Three Methods of Representing Change," *Research in Higher Education*, Vol. 33, No. 1, 1992, pp. 71–83.

Portes, Alejando, and Min Zhou, "Should Immigrants Assimilate," *Public Interest*, Vol. 116, Summer 1994, pp. 18–33.

President's Task Force on Multicultural Education and Campus Diversity, *The Challenge of Diversity and Multicultural Education*, Long Beach, Calif.: California State University, Long Beach, January 1991.

Pruitt, France J., "The Adaptation of African Students to American Society," *International Journal of Multicultural Relations*, Vol. 2, 1978, pp. 90–118.

Richardson, Richard C., Jr., and Louis W. Bender, "Students in Urban Settings: Achieving the Baccalaureate Degree," *AHSE-ERIC Higher Education Report No. 6*, Washington, D.C.: The Association for the Study of Higher Education, 1985.

Richardson, Richard C., Jr., and Elizabeth Fisk Skinner, *Achieving Quality and Diversity: Universities in a Multicultural Society*, Washington, D.C.: American Council on Education, 1991.

Romero, Migdalia, *Roundtable Report on Immigrant Issues in Higher Education*, prepared for The Andrew W. Mellon Foundation, New York, 1991.

Roos, Peter D., "Postsecondary Plyler IHELG Monograph 91-7," Houston: Institute of Education Law and Governance, University of Houston Law Center, 1991.

Scarpaci, Joseph L., and Sandra H. Fradd, "Latin-Americans at the University Level: Implications for Instruction," *Journal of Multicultural Counseling and Development*, Vol. 13, 1985, pp. 183–189.

Schmidtlein, Frank A., "Administrative Structures and Decision-Making Processes," Marvin W. Peterson and Lisa A. Mets, eds., *Key Resources on Higher Education Governance, Management, and Leadership: A Guide to the Literature*, San Francisco, Calif.: Jossey-Bass, 1987, pp. 139–162.

Searles, W., and C. Ward, "Prediction of Psychological and Sociocultural Adjustment During Cross-Cultural Transitions," *International Journal of Intercultural Relations*, 1990, pp. 449–464.

Senate Office of Research, *Californians Together: Defining the State's Role in Immigration*, Sacramento, Calif.: Senate Office of Research, July 1993.

Shih, Frank H., "Asian-American Students: The Myth of a Model Minority," *Journal of College Science Teaching*, 1988, pp. 356–359.

Shires, Michael A., *The Master Plan Revisited (Again): Prospects for Providing Access to Public Undergraduate Education in California*, Santa Monica, Calif.: RAND, DRU-965-LE, 1995.

Silvesti, G., and J. M. Lukasiewicz, "A Look at Occupational Employment Trends to the Year 2000," *Bureau of Labor Statistics Monthly Labor Reviews*, November 1989.

Sodowsky, Gargi R., and John C. Carey, "Asian Indian Immigrants in America: Factors Related to Adjustments," *Journal of Multicultural Counseling and Development*, Vol. 15, 1987, pp. 129–141.

Stewart, Jocelyn Y., "Remedial California State Students Blame School System," *Los Angeles Times*, January 8, 1995, pp. B1 and B4.

Stodt, Martha M., and William M. Klepper, "Increasing Retention: Academic and Student Affairs Administrators in Partnership," *New*

Directions for Higher Education Number 60, San Francisco, Calif.: Jossey-Bass, 1987.

Sue, Stanley, and Nolan W. S. Zane, "Academic Achievement and Socioemotional Adjustment Among Chinese University Students," *Journal of Counseling Psychology*, Vol. 32, No. 4, 1985, pp. 570–579.

Tinto, Vincent, *Leaving College*, Chicago: University of Chicago Press, 1987.

U.S. Department of Justice, *1990 Statistical Yearbook of the Immigration and Naturalization Service*, Washington, D.C.: U.S. Government Printing Office, December 1991.

U.S. Department of Labor, *The Effects of Immigration on the U.S. Economy and Labor Market*, Washington, D.C.: Bureau of International Labor Affairs, May 1989.

University of California Latino Eligibility Task Force, *Latino Student Eligibility and Participation in the University of California: Report Number One of the Latino Eligibility Task Force*, Santa Cruz, Calif.: University of California Latino Eligibility Task Force, Division of Social Sciences, University of California, Santa Cruz, March 1993.

Vernez, Georges, and Allan Abrahamse, *How Immigrants Fare in U.S. Education*, Santa Monica, Calif.: RAND, MR-718-AMF, 1996.

Vernez, Georges, and Kevin McCarthy, *Meeting the Economy's Labor Needs Through Immigration: Rationale and Challenges*, Santa Monica, Calif.: RAND, N-3052-FF, 1990.

Wallace, Amy, "California State Takes Step to Cut Remedial Classes," *Los Angeles Times*, January 26, 1995, pp. A3 and A19.

Warren, Robert, *Estimates of the Unauthorized Immigrant Population Residing in the United States, by Country of Origin and State of Residence: October, 1992*, Washington, D.C.: Immigration and Naturalization Service, April 1994.

Weber, Arnold R., "Higher Education, Public Concerns, and Institutional Angst," The Aspen Institute, ed., *American Higher Education: Purposes, Problems and Public Perceptions*, Queenstown, Md.:   The Aspen Institute, Program in Education for a Changing Society, 1992, pp. 201–217.

Weick, Carol, "Educational Organizations as Loosely Coupled Systems," *Administrative Science Quarterly*, Vol. 25, March 1976, pp. 1–19.

Woo, Elaine, "Immigrants Do Well in School, Study Finds," *Los Angeles Times*, April, 3, 1995, pp. A1 and A8.

Yin, Robert K., *Case Study Research: Design and Methods*, Second Edition, Thousand Oaks, Calif.: Sage, 1994.

Zook, Jim, "Pell Grant Protest: Proposal to Bar Use for English-as-a-Second-Language Training Raises Concern," *The Chronicle of Higher Education*, September 21, 1994, p. A35.

Zumeta, William, and Janet Looney, "State Policy and Budget Developments," National Education Association (NEA), ed., *The NEA 1994 Almanac of Higher Education*, Washington, D.C.: NEA, 1994, pp. 79–103.